THE GOLF CLUB

400 YEARS OF THE GOOD, THE BEAUTIFUL & THE CREATIVE

JEFFERY B. ELLIS

ZEPHYR PRODUCTIONS, INC.

Layout designed by: Don Bull Creative, #25 - 2156 West 12th Avenue, Vancouver, British Columbia, Canada. V6K 2N2

Edited by: Saundra Sheffer, 1422 Calle Linda, San Dimas, California 91773

Photography by Jeffery B. Ellis except for the Troon clubs—photographs courtesy of Robert Pringle; and the Robert T. Jones, Jr. Calamity Jane putter, the Alan Shepard moon club, and the Edinburgh Cleek Club presentation iron photographs courtesy of the USGA.

This book may be ordered directly from the publisher.
Published by:
Zephyr Productions, Inc.
P.O. Box 1964
Oak Harbor, WA 98277
Phone (Toll Free): 1-888-394-9333

Attention golf clubs, golf companies, corporations, and businesses:
Quantity discounts are available on bulk purchases of this book for educational training purposes, fund-raising, or gift giving.

Library of Congress Control Number: 2002103717

ISBN 0-9653039-2-6 (Hardcover Edition)
ISBN 0-9653039-3-4 (Limited Edition)

2002103717
CIP

10 9 8 7 6 5 4 3 2 1

Printed in China

DEDICATION

To my wife Susan
and my daughter Leah,

I remain forever the lucky one.

UNKNOWN MAKER
LIGHT IRON
CIRCA 1600s

UNKNOWN MAKER
HEAVY IRON
CIRCA 1800

BRIDGEPORT GUN IMPLEMENT CO.
MASHIE
CIRCA 1900

WHITCOME DELUXE
JW GAUDIN 5-IRON
CIRCA 1930

WILSON
STAFF DYNA-POWER 5-IRON
1965

PING
I3 5-IRON
2001

UNKNOWN MAKER
SCRAPER
CIRCA 1750

HUGH PHILP
MIDDLE SPOON
CIRCA 1840

ROBERT ANDERSON
DRIVER
1891

SPALDING
H. CARSON DRIVER

CIRCA 1925

MACGREGOR
TOMMY ARMOUR 693 DRIVER

1949

CALLAWAY
BIGGEST BIG BERTHA DRIVER

1997

ANDREW DICKSON
PUTTER

CIRCA 1750

HUGH PHILP
PUTTER

CIRCA 1850

WILLIE PARK, JR.
PUTTER

CIRCA 1890

MACGREGOR
TOMMY ARMOUR PUTTER
CIRCA 1935

PING
ANSER PUTTER
1966

ODYSSEY
ROSSIE II PUTTER
1994

FORWARD

When I began working at the United States Golf Association's Museum and Archives in the late 1980's, my first assignment was to inventory and catalog the extensive collection of antique golf clubs. As I started the project, I had to admit that my knowledge of golf clubs made prior to the Jimmy Carter era was scant — and that may be generous. Nonetheless, there was something magical about the moment when I opened that first box of clubs in the museum's attic storage area, and peered in among the tangle of wooden shafts, iron clubheads, and brown leather grips. One by one, each club that I pulled from the box and turned over slowly in my hands began to tell a story. A deep gouge in the face of a wooden clubhead, a split shaft repaired with care, a leather grip built up with layers of woolen listing to fit a meaty hand — the physical attributes and features documented the unique history of each club. • Such clubs are not simply sentimental fossils of ages past, but almost sacred relics that enable us to connect physically with the game's heroes and traditions. Everybody can appreciate the warmth and charm of an antique brassey spoon, the perfect balance of a well-crafted lofter, and the romance of a wood-shafted putter. Then when one discovers that the brassey spoon was crafted by a British Open champion, that the lofter was born without the use of electricity, and that the putter is an exact duplicate of the one Bob Jones used to win the Grand Slam, the game comes alive in a way unlike any other. • Recognizing that few individuals are so blessed as to have such ready access to a comprehensive collection of antique golf clubs, we are fortunate that the game's literature includes some splendid books that document the history of the golf club and the clubmakers who produced them. Chief among these is Jeff Ellis's *The Clubmaker's Art: Antique Golf Clubs and Their History* (1997), an authoritative and indispensable reference. Ellis earned the deepest admiration of golfers and golf historians alike for the scholarship and artistry that make *The Clubmaker's Art* so impressive. To more than a handful of people I have related my opinion that *The Clubmaker's Art* is one of the five or six most important works on the history of the game. Picking up where *The Clubmaker's Art* leaves off, *The Golf Club: 400 Years of The Good, The Beautiful, and The Creative* documents the evolution of the golf club throughout the entire history of the game. • It was with great pleasure, therefore, that I accepted Jeff's request to pen this introduction to his latest contribution to the library of golf. *The Golf Club* presents an impressive visual history of the game's essential tools, accompanied by the impeccable research that demonstrates Jeff's passion for golf history. You will surely find among these pages more than a few clubs that will bring to life the legends of the game. I trust that you will enjoy this book as much as I have.

Rand Jerris, Ph.D.
Director, USGA Museum and Archives

PREFACE

Golfers from every era have sought to achieve the same thing—improvement. They want to hit the ball farther, straighter, and more accurately. In golf the lower the score, the better. This fact motivates the beginning golfer as well as the seasoned professional to practice, but inevitably their attention turns to their equipment. Might a new driver hit the ball five yards further? Could new irons remedy that hook or slice? Maybe a new putter will vanquish the dreaded 3-putt. • A study of the golf club, from the oldest to the newest, shows creative minds at work. Across the years, a wide variety of clubs were made with the goal of solving the golfer's problems, but alas, most did not, at least not to the desired extent. Still, golfers continue to search for clubs that will help them play just a little better and clubmakers continue to create new implements designed to do just that. • Delving into the history of golf clubs brings to life many of the great characters that shaped today's game, and it is clear that golfers from every era shared the same joys and frustrations that golfers do today. Many modern "innovations" are merely variations on a theme explored long ago during the wood shaft era. Truly, the golf club is a fascinating implement which reveals much about the golfer's eternal quest for a competitive advantage. • Nowhere in the world is there a public display that chronicles the evolution of the golf club in great breadth and depth. The reason for this is simple: early, historical, unusual, and visually captivating examples are extremely hard to come by. It is to simulate such a collection that I have written this book. I did not include every clubmaker or every golf club innovation, but I did strive to provide a representative cross-section of clubs that tell the unique story of human ingenuity as applied to golf. • In creating this book, I received much help. I would like to thank the following individuals: Steve Bain, David Berkowitz, Roger Cleveland, Dave Counsell, Dick Donovan, Dick Hartshorne, Laurie Hodulick, Dennis Hucul, Rand Jerris, Ron John, Jim Leaptrott, Susan and George Lewis, Debbi Mathews, Kevin McGrath, Andy Mutch, Chris Saxman, Jack Stiltz, John Solheim, Pat Sutton, Mike Waller, Ronnie Watts, Tom Wishon, and Chris Zimmerman. Thank you to Mike Fields and Frank McNab for allowing me to photograph clubs from their respective pro shops. Thank you also to the United States Golf Association for providing three images of clubs from their museum, and to Robert Pringle for providing the images of the Troon Clubs. Special thanks to the following for allowing me to photograph items from their respective collections: Rick Almberg, Gene Bolden, Lance and Danielle Enholm, Jim Espinola, Dick Estey, Bing Kunzig, Jim Leaptrott, Tad Moore, and Al Whalen. A huge debt of gratitude to Don Bull of Don Bull Creative, Vancouver, British Columbia, for the layout design of this book and to Saundra Sheffer, San Dimas, California, for her tireless editing and brilliant suggestions. I would also like to acknowledge my family—my wife, Susan; my kids, Meredith, Scott, Leah, and Katie; my siblings, Les, Stephen, and Joan; and my mom—for their tireless support, encouragement, and tolerance.

J. B. E.

GOLF CLUBS

AS COLLECTIBLES

People who own old golf clubs often wonder if their clubs are worth money, and, if so, how much. They know that old things are sometimes worth a princely sum. Even so, most old golf clubs are not of great value, at least not yet. But to speak only of current value is to overlook important characteristics that old golf clubs possess. It is because of these elements that some clubs are eventually reborn as collectibles. Golf clubs made during the wood shaft era are collectible for four basic reasons. First, they are old. Wood was the first material used to make a golf shaft, and the wood shaft era ended early in the 20th century. Owning a wood shaft golf club provides the contemporary golfer with a physical connection to the game as it was played in the first part of the 20th century and hundreds of years before. Second, old wood shaft clubs are historical. Not only were most of the "improvements" seen in golf clubs today pioneered in wood shaft clubs, many creative and visually interesting features were tried only in the wood shaft era. The position of early wood shaft clubs in history is secure; nothing came before them, and their number is finite. Third, antique wood shaft clubs are aesthetically pleasing. There is a warmth and richness to wood that steel and graphite do not possess. A number of the old wood shaft clubs show such fine workmanship and creativity that they look more like works of art than utilitarian implements. Fourth, they represent a lost art. The craftsmen who made these clubs were true artisans. Much of the work, if not all, was done by hand. Mass production, investment casting, injection molding, milling machines, computers, and CAD (Computer Assisted Draw) programs did not exist back then. Prior to the 1890s, clubmakers did not even use electricity.

Not all wood shaft clubs are equal in the eyes of collectors. Only the oldest clubs (those made before 1890) and the most unusual clubs (those with a dramatically different structural feature) draw high prices. The vast bulk of the remaining wood shaft clubs are similar in appearance, offering little to entice the collector to prefer one over another. Hence, the values for common hickory shaft clubs is still relatively low. As a group, however, old wood shaft clubs are sought after, and their values continue to rise. Clubs with steel and other types of modern shafts do not have the same legacy as wood shaft clubs. They are, however, much better to use. As playable clubs they certainly have value, and some golfers spend a lot of money, time, and effort to get clubs that fit their personal requirements. Very few models, however, are worth more now than when they were first sold, which is understandable. There was a time, however, when many contemporary models were briefly considered desirable and exceedingly valuable collectibles. In the 1980s, Lee Trevino, Greg Norman, Ben Crenshaw, and a host of other top touring pros still preferred the persimmon head woods made in the 1950s. Even the great Jack Nicklaus used persimmon woods into the late 1980s, specifically, a MacGregor 945 Eye-O-Matic driver (1953-1954) and a MacGregor 693 3-wood (1949-1952). When the golfing public saw the best golfers in the world using woods made 20 to 35 years earlier, they wanted their own classic woods. This hero worship created a huge secondary market in which persimmon woods—as well as a few specific wedges, putters, and iron sets from this era—were resold for serious money. The capital of this secondary market was Tokyo, Japan. Because Japanese dealers purchased their inventory in the U.S., the stateside values of many of these classic clubs jumped dramatically: $4000 for a mint set of MacGregor 693's, $2,500 for a Tommy Armour

IMG5 putter, $750 for a 1958 Wilson Dyna-Powered sand wedge. But these values did not last. The reasons for the rise in classic club values—hero worship and perceived playability—were also the reason for the collapse that occurred in the early 1990s. New heroes began to dominate the top of the money list, and they were using clubs based on new technology. Rarity (which is different from availability) was never the reason for the increase in classic club values, since all the desirable models were mass produced by the hundreds, thousands, and tens of thousands within the last few decades, and most still exist. Only a handful of classic clubs from the 1950s-60s have retained a value well above that of an ordinary used club. There are, however, steel shaft clubs made during the mid 20th century and thereafter that possess significant creativity and genuine beauty as well as elements of nostalgia and history. These intrinsic properties are more durable criteria for collecting than intangibles so fickle as hero worship, playability, or current demand. The number of steel shaft clubs manufactured runs well into the billions. Hence the vast majority of steel shaft clubs are valued merely as used clubs once they hit the secondary market. Their value continues to drop as newer, more modern equipment, takes center stage. This is not all bad, however. Steel shaft clubs can be collected at very reasonable prices. The collector simply needs to be judicious when collecting steel shaft clubs and have a clear focus on what it is that he or she is looking for or desires. Today there are modern clubs which emphasize a collectible element and command a sizable price. Many of these are beautiful clubs with outstanding playability. A golfer who likes such a club and finds the price acceptable is probably getting a good deal. It just might be the club of his or her dreams. Golfers who want to collect, however, should take a long-range view of the market and try to determine if there is, indeed, a genuine basis for collectibility. It should be obvious that something recently fabricated to appeal to the collectibles market is not as meaningful as something that was artfully crafted years ago in a genuine effort to improve the game, solve a fault, or enhance play. In the long run, it is a club's place in history and innovative creativity—rather than "instant collectibility"—that determines whether it will stand the test of time. To help the reader understand a little more about the values of various golf clubs, actually transaction prices have been included with some of the clubs shown in this book. Very few steel shaft clubs include prices because very few of them currently sell for more than their value as a used club. Condition is critical to the value of a collectible golf club. Because steel shaft clubs have been produced in such large numbers, they should be in outstanding original condition in order to increase their chances of appreciating in value. A wood shaft club should also be free from significant damage or blemishes in order to be considered a top example, although a moderate amount of wear and tear is often acceptable. Just as a collectible coin may have a wide range of values depending on condition, so, too, does a collectible golf club. The best collection is that in which the collector builds his or her collection with items they enjoy—whatever those items may be. Such a collection will provide great personal satisfaction and acquire a distinction all its own.

LIST OF GOLF BALLS ILLUSTRATED

TABLE OF CONTENTS

The origin of the golf club, like the origin of the game itself, is lost in the mists of antiquity. Perhaps it was a shepherd's crook turned upside down or a branch with a slight bend at its end. Some historians speculate that the most likely prospect was a young thorn tree sprouting from the side of a hill. The trunk would soon curve skyward thereby forming the needed angle between shaft and head when cut for use. The head, being near the root, would be quite dense and hard; the shaft would be durable and appropriately thick to hold on to. • The oldest existing clubs are generally thought to date from the 1600s if not the 1500s. The oldest written reference to golf, however, dates to 1457, when golf was declared illegal in the Black Acts of Scotland. The King's soldiers were apparently spending too much time playing golf and not enough time practicing their archery. Centuries would pass before England and Scotland would use golf balls to vie for superiority. • The earliest remaining clubs are found as both woods and irons. Unlike today, the golfer carried more woods than irons, since they typically used wooden head clubs from tee to cup. Irons were used primarily to extract a ball from surroundings that might damage a wooden head. • Early woods are quite large, having a long head that often measures 6 inches or more between the tip of the toe and the back of the neck. This "long nose" shape remained the standard for all woods until approximately 1890. There are, however, individual characteristics that are peculiar to each era. • Early irons are also quite large and sometimes extremely heavy. The earliest irons can be recognized by the squared-off toe. The early blacksmith or armorer would make the head by heating and hammering a rectangular bar of metal into shape, ignoring the nicety of rounding off the square end of the clubhead. The rounded toe we know today, however, became the standard by approximately 1800. By 1800 there were only 15 golf clubs (societies) in the world and very few golfers. Clubs (implements) made before 1800 are, obviously, the hardest to find, as all the known examples could fit comfortably into two golf bags. • The golf ball used during this period consisted of three pieces of leather sewn together then stuffed with feathers. They served the purpose, but left plenty of room for improvement. Feather balls were susceptible to moisture, liable to split open, and were seldom perfectly round. Feather balls came in various sizes and weights.

The six woods and two irons of the "Troon clubs" are considered by many historians to be the oldest known golf clubs. It is generally believed that these clubs date to the 1600s if not the 1500s. All of the clubs are stamped many times with a unique mark. The woods are stamped on the top of their heads, and the irons are stamped on the shafts. The mark consists of an oval, pointed at both ends, enclosing a crown in the upper area, a Scotch thistle in the lower area, a five-pointed star in the center, a letter "C" to the right of the star, and the letter "I" (or "J") to the left of the star. The initials may be those of the maker, and the crown and thistle may denote a special appointment given to the clubmaker by a Scottish king. Or, the marks could simply denote ownership.

The Troon woods, consisting of drivers and spoons, are characterized by a long head with a very distinct point at the toe, lead that protrudes from the back of the head, a thick piece of horn on the sole, an ash shaft, and knots in the wood. There are a light iron and a heavy iron. Only the heavy iron has a "spur" on the toe. The spur was used to dislodge a ball lying in a rut or among stones by striking it with the end of the toe. A spur on the light iron would be superfluous since the heavy iron had one. In 1999 the Troon Golf Club voted to refuse an offer of $4 million for their eight clubs. Instead, the Club decided to allow the clubs to remain on display at the St. Andrews Golf Museum.

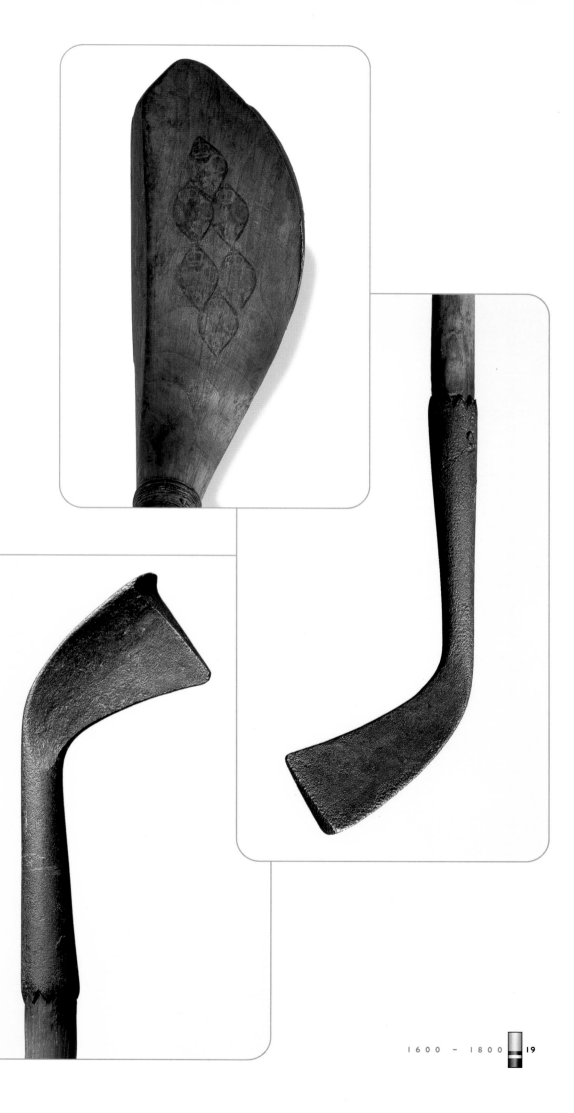

SPUR TOE IRON

Heavy Irons, as they were known in their day, were designed for use when the ball was deep among stones or in mud. Notice the thickness and length of the hosel on this heavy iron. Its massive size and weight insured the extraction of the ball, not great distance. This late 1600s spur toe iron is one of only six known examples. Owned by the Earl of Wemyss, this club is the companion to a light iron sold by Bonhams auction house in 1998 for approximately $250,000.

DICKSON PUTTER

Stamped "A.D.", this putter was made by Andrew Dickson of Leith, Scotland. Dickson is mentioned as a clubmaker in Thomas Mathison's 1743 work *The Goff*. Dickson was known to mark his clubs with just his initials "A.D." "James McCaul" is also stamped into the head. During the 1890s and early 1900s, McCaul was a prominent Scottish golfer who acquired this club and marked it with his name—not an uncommon practice. A small circular sticker on the ash shaft is marked "GIE 1901," evidence of the club's inclusion in the 1901 Glasgow International Exhibition. The only other club attributed to Dickson sold privately in 2000 for $380,000.

SCRAPER

In 1790 *Hoyle's Games Improved* described the different types of long nose clubs as "the Common Club, used when the Ball lies on good Ground; the Scraper and Half Scraper, when in long Grass, and the Spoon, when in a Hollow." This circa 1750 club is a Scraper. The large amount of lead that protrudes from the back, as well as three lead plugs visible on the sole, makes this a heavy club. The extra weight would have been helpful when striking a ball in high grass. A similar wood dating from the mid 1700s, complete with protruding lead backweight and a woollen listing grip like the one on this club, sold at the 2001 International Golf Auction held at Sloan's in Miami, Florida, for $150,000.

SQUARE TOE IRON

Light irons, as they were called, were designed primarily for use when the ball lay on sandy ground or among small stones. This circa 1600s light iron is nearly identical in design, shape, size, and style to the Troon light iron. They differ only in the style of their nicking.

SQUARE TOE IRON

Complete with its original alder shaft, this circa 1700 square toe heavy iron is somewhat different in structure from the square toe irons presented on the previous pages. The Troon irons have a blade that sweeps up into the hosel, as does the square toe iron on page 21. The spur toe iron on page 20 has a much smaller sweep. This club, however, has no sweep at all. Instead, there is a sharp crease where the blade meets the hosel. Irons constructed in this manner date as far back as the late 1600s. This iron is an early example of a second generation square toe iron. It has sharp corners at the end of the toe and shows the blackish brown patina found on the earliest irons. Notice the square nail in the hosel. It was used to help attach the head to the shaft. In 1992, this club sold at a Phillips auction in Edinburgh for approximately $100,000.

MIDDLE SPOON

Just as irons between 1600 and 1800 came in two basic types—square toe and round toe—woods crafted during this time also came in two types: long/slender and bulbous/stocky. Dating to the late 1700s, this wood is of the bulbous variety. It has a distinctly broad, rounded head and a thick neck. In 1999 Bonhams in Manchester, England, auctioned this club for nearly $50,000.

SQUARE TOE IRON

Dating to the mid 1700s, this square toe heavy iron was once the property of the Royal Perth Golf Club. In 1998, Royal Perth auctioned off the bulk of their golf antiques to pay for repairs and alterations to their course, which had been prone to flooding in years past. The sale raised well over $750,000. Sold at auction by Christie's in Glasgow, Scotland, this particular club accounted for $75,000 of the total.

COSSAR PLAY CLUB

Simon and his son David Cossar made clubs in Leith, Scotland, between 1785, when Simon entered the trade, and 1816, when David followed Simon, his father, in death. They were the first clubmakers to mark their work with their entire last name. Only four marked Cossar clubs are known, although replicas abound. This slender Cossar play club sold privately in 2000 for $300,000.

SQUARE TOE IRON

This circa 1780 square toe iron is neither large and heavy enough to be a heavy iron nor small and light enough to be a light iron. During its day, it was termed a "middling iron" according to a description of clubs in use in 1805. This description, found in an 1805 St. Andrews court deposition, identifies the middling iron along with the iron club and light iron. In 1992 this club sold at a Sporting Antiquities auction in Boston for $77,000

ROUND TOE IRON

Early irons were entirely handmade by blacksmiths or, on rare occasion, armorers. Beginning with a rectangular bar of iron, the smithy would heat and hammer out the bar, eventually working it into a clubhead. Evidence of its handmade nature is found all over this late 1700s round toe middle iron. The face still has numerous indentations left by the blacksmith's hammer. On the side of the neck is a visible seam (created when forming the hosel around a mandrel), and the face and hosel are anything but symmetrical.

McEWAN MIDDLE SPOON

James McEwan began making clubs in 1770. A number of his descendants also became clubmakers and continued the family business in Edinburgh for over 120 years. The earliest McEwan clubs were marked with a thistle, the emblem of Scotland. This circa 1800 club does not have the thistle, but it does have the same distinctive "McEwan" stamp that is found on those clubs with the thistle.

ROUND TOE IRON

This circa 1800 heavy iron, formerly owned by the Duke of Athole, might look rather ordinary. But don't let the picture fool you. It is massive, as were all early heavy irons. The club itself weighs over a pound and a half! Notice the round toe. As the craft of making irons progressed, blacksmiths began to take the extra steps needed to round off the toe. This made the iron look more finished and removed the two pointed corners which could damage the wooden head clubs when carried about by golfer or caddie. This was a concern as indicated by the occasional square toe with its corners filed off.

Between 1800 and 1850, both woods and irons underwent a period of refinement. Clubmakers were beginning to consider how to improve their product to help golfers lower their scores. • During this time, irons were downsized. Those made in 1850 were significantly smaller than their counterparts made in 1800. The hosel was not as thick or as long, nor the blade as deep and concave. These changes made the iron lighter and easier to swing. Allan Robertson, the first golfer in history to break 80, is credited with being the first to play his approach shots with an iron, beginning in 1848. • Long nose woods kept their same basic shape, but went from blocky and utilitarian to sleek and graceful. By 1850, necks had changed from big and thick to thin and delicate. Faces were much shallower, usually measuring only one inch in depth. Overall, the long nose club made in 1850 had beautiful lines with the best examples displaying a genuine elegance. • It was during this period that long nose clubmakers began to mark their work. Of the 14 known clubmakers working prior to 1800, only Andrew Dickson, James McEwan, and the Cossars (Simon and David) are known to have marked their work, and then only towards the late 1700s. By 1850 it was standard procedure for the major long nose clubmakers to mark their work. • Wooden clubs of this era were made in a number of different varieties. The most common were the play club or driver, long spoon, middle spoon, short spoon, baffing spoon, driving putter, and putter. The play club or driver was used to put the ball in play off the tee. It had the longest shaft and, outside of the putter, the least amount of loft. The long, middle, short, and baffing spoons were used through the green from normal grassy lies. The shaft length corresponds with the club's name, except for the baffing spoon which was at least as short as a short spoon. The faces usually increase in loft as the shaft decreases in length. Driving putters were designed to play long putts or to drive a ball low against a heavy wind. They were not as upright as an ordinary putter, and their shafts were neither as long as a play club nor as short as a putter. • The feather ball remained in use during this period. They were expensive to buy because a feather ball maker could produce only three to nine balls a day. The difference in number produced was most likely determined by the quality of construction, the state of the raw materials used, and the skill of the ball maker. In 1845, Robert A. Patterson molded a golf ball from gutta percha, and it was used on the links of St. Andrews. By 1850 the gutta percha ball was on its way to replacing the feather ball.

JACKSON BAFFING SPOON

In 1825, when only 20 years old, John Jackson began working for the Perth Golfing Society in Perth, Scotland. He proved to be a fine craftsman, and he remained a clubmaker until his death in 1878. His early work, characterized by beautiful sweeping lines and graceful curves, is often compared to that of Hugh Philp. However, far fewer examples of Jackson's work remain. This Jackson baffing spoon, designed for short approach shots, dates to approximately 1830-35. It sold at a 1991 Sotheby's auction, in Chester, England, for $32,000.

BELL PLAY CLUB

While working as keeper of the green at Dalhousie Golf Club in Carnoustie, Scotland, Frank Bell was censured for keeping a pig on the grounds and for letting his dog run about. He was also criticized for his green-keeping. As a clubmaker, however, Bell was a craftsman of superior ability, as the graceful lines of this circa 1850 play club testify.

P.G. BAFFING SPOON

This early 1800s baffing spoon was designed for short approach shots. Irons during this era were used primarily when the ball lay among unfriendly elements, such as stones, sand, or high grass. The only marks on this club are the initials "P.G.," which are most likely those of the owner.

JAMESON PUTTER

Just as there are unmarked clubs made by unknown clubmakers, there are clubs marked with the names of makers unknown to the world today. This putter, marked J. Jameson is one such club. It is unfortunate that not all clubmakers were documented, but, over 150 years ago when this club was made, the old Scottish clubmakers didn't really care whether they were documented or not. Getting paid was of far greater interest!

McEWAN PUTTER

This McEwan putter was originally made as a prize or presentation club. It is pictured and described in the March 1916 issue of *The American Golfer*. According to the article, this putter dates to 1800 and was originally collected by the Rev. Robert Forgan of St. Andrews, son of Robert Forgan the clubmaker. The Burke Golf Company asked to borrow this club and others that belonged to Rev. Forgan for their display at a golf exhibition in San Francisco. The Reverend ultimately sold the clubs to the Burke Golf Company.

This circa 1825 putter has a feature not often found in early clubs: It is left-handed. The early clubmaker did not enjoy making a left-handed golf club. To do so required the maker to reverse his methods and procedures when crafting the clubhead. This required a great deal of painstaking labor.

APPROACH IRON

This circa 1800 iron (shown actual size) has a shallow but extremely thick blade. It also has a relatively short (36 1/2 inches) shaft and a distinct upright lie. If it didn't have such a lofted blade, it would be easy to classify this club as a putter; however, a putter it is not. According to an account published in the October 8, 1842, *Chambers Edinburgh Journal*, this club is the earliest of "cleeks" and was designed for striking a ball out of a rough or grassy place when near the hole. Hence, the short shaft and upright lie. The 1930s tee is shown for perspective.

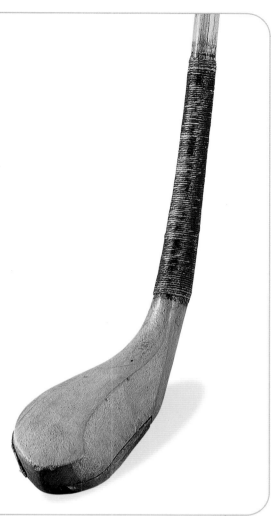

SHORT SPOON

Long nose woods made prior to 1850 were often left unmarked by their maker. The example above, with its unrefined workmanship and dramatically curved face, is one such club. It is unmarked and dates well before 1850.

PHILP MIDDLE SPOON

Born in 1782, Hugh Philp was the clubmaker to the R&A from 1817 until his death in 1856. His meticulous nature was legendary. His work became the standard by which the work of all other clubmakers was measured. His craftsmanship was compared to that of Stradivarius, and golfers advertised to collect his clubs over 100 years ago. Forty-four years after his death, *Golf Illustrated* reported that a Philp club was worth untold gold. Today, his legend continues unabated.

TRACK IRON

Early golf was played mostly on courses near the sea. The locals would cross the course when traveling to the beach and leave tracks which the golfer had to deal with. Track irons were devised to strike a golf ball in a cart track, horseshoe print, or ruts of various types. The small circular head allowed the club to fit into tight spots. The large heavy hosel provided considerable weight and, therefore, momentum.

DUNN PLAY CLUB

Willie Dunn is one of golf's best-known figures from the nineteenth century. He played in many a challenge match against the other great names of his time: Willie Park, Allan Robertson, and Tom Morris. One of his most unusual matches was a winner-take-all *twenty*-round match against Allan Robertson played in ten days. Dunn lost 2 down with 1 to play. This late 1840s left-handed play club was sold by Christie's in 1995 for $20,000.

PHILP LONG SPOON

This circa 1840 Philp long spoon is one of only five known examples marked "H. Philp" in script. It is thought that Hugh used his script stamp to identify either his personal clubs or the presentation/prize clubs he made for a particular person or occasion. During the feather ball era, clubs were sometimes the prize in a competition.

PHILP PUTTER

This presentation putter is beautifully engraved with a ringed cross, actually a Celtic cross—the religious symbol of the Scots and other Celtic peoples. It is not known why Philp chose (or was instructed) to engrave one of his clubs with this symbol. It was, however, a symbol that any Scottish golfer would welcome on his putter. The Celtic cross was the symbol the Scotts carried into battle. Only three engraved long nose presentation clubs are known: two McEwans and this Philp.

MCEWAN LONG SPOON

This circa 1840 McEwan long spoon
possesses many of the traits of a Philp club
from the same era. Note the long, slender
head, the slender neck, and the shallow
face. These are three elements Philp
incorporated into his work.

HEAVY IRON

This circa 1800 round toe heavy iron has a
large dished face and a hosel that measures
6 inches in length. Such a large iron head
made for a very hefty club. This one has a
dead weight of over 23 ounces. The name
of the maker is not known. His work, however, is easily recognized by the ornamental
ring cut around the top of the hosel, so he
is simply referred to as "the ringmaker." Six
examples of his work are known. In 2000
a ringmaker heavy iron similar to this one
sold at a Phillips auction in England for just
under $40,000. Note: the tee shown
is not from this era, but has been
included for perspective.

IRON

With a head shaped like a track iron but much larger in size, this circa 1800 iron was displayed at the Glasgow Exhibition of 1911. Each club displayed in the 1911 exhibition has a long, rectangular, yellow label on the shaft near the grip. This club has one. The featherball, of normal size, shows the massive size of this iron.

McEWAN PUTTER

Putters were generally used within 30 yards of the hole to play the ball into the hole. Sometimes, depending on the terrain and wind, they were used outside of 30 yards. This McEwan putter dates to the 1840s.

DUPLEX WOOD

Designed for both right- and left-handed use, this duplex wood dates to the early 1800s. In the early 1900s, this unique club came into the possession of Harry C. Wood, the noted author of *Golfing Curios and the Like* published in 1910. Wood's yellow identification tag still hangs high on the shaft. Wood's collection was sold in 1986, and this club was purchased privately one year later for $23,000.

IRON PUTTER

Iron putters, or putting cleeks, did not come into vogue until the 1890s. The odd iron putter was tried earlier, but it was ridiculed and never recommended. As pictured, this early 1800s putter might look ordinary, but it is not. This clubhead is massive. Notice the huge 6-inch long hosel, the thick blade, and the large sawtooth nicking atop the hosel. These crude features are traits of truly old irons. The only iron putter of this vintage to sell in recent years was auctioned by Christie's in 1998 for $175,000. This example belongs to the Los Angeles Country Club and is on display there.

PHILP PUTTER

This unused Hugh Philp putter was once part of an unused set of nine Philp clubs presented by Sir Hew Dalrymple, Bart., of Lucie, to John E. Laidlay, a two-time British Amateur champion. Recognized as one of a kind, Laidlay's set was displayed inside its own glass case at the 1901 Glasgow International Exhibition. In 1981 this set was split up, each club selling individually at a Sotheby's auction in London. This putter drew the highest price—a mere $5,000.

Between 1850 and 1870, both irons and woods went through significant changes. Irons continued to evolve and downsize. Heavy and light irons were replaced by lofters and cleeks, respectively. Unlike early irons, cleeks and lofters were sometimes used to approach the green. The cleek was designed more for distance, while the lofter was designed to elevate the ball, especially on short approach shots. • During this period the track iron came into vogue. Similar clubs had been devised decades earlier, but they were not widely used. Track irons had a heavy, round head just slightly larger than the ball itself. They were used when the ball landed in a narrow cart rut, horseshoe or other indentation in the ground, in thick or stiff whins, or in any round, deep hollow that was not completely beyond the player's reach. • Unlike the irons made during this period, which were evolving towards greater utility, woods were being constructed with an eye toward increased durability. Clubmakers began to make faces a little deeper and necks a bit thicker, as the gutty ball, which began to replace the feather ball in the late 1840s, caused greater wear and tear to the clubhead. (During the feather ball era, when the club and ball made contact, the ball was more likely to break or suffer damage than the club.) Increasing the mass of a clubhead improved its durability, but it did not make the club more attractive. The sleek, slender heads made by Hugh Philp and others at the end of the featherball era were casualties of the harder ball and other changes in the game. • In 1860, the first Open Championship was held. In its early years, this tournament, known in the U.S. as the British Open, was usually won by a professional who was also a clubmaker. Since the golf population was still small, only a few craftsmen were able to earn a living by making golf clubs full time. To improve their financial stability, many clubmakers sought work as golf professionals, hiring on as a course custodian or keeper of the green. But, those wages, too, were modest, so many professionals did it all—kept the greens, gave lessons, made and repaired clubs, and played matches against other professionals for prize money on the side. • By 1850, the gutty ball, not the feather ball, was dominating the golf ball market. Gutta percha, a gum derived from various Malaysian trees, was easier to make, less expensive to buy, and, as time proved, better to golf with. Initially gutta percha balls were made smooth, similar to feather balls, but it was quickly learned that a used, marked-up ball flew much better than a new one. Consequently, ballmakers began to mark the surface of the ball before it was sold. Patterns were usually cut into the surface of the ball by hand until the mid 1870s, when golf ball cutting lathes came into prominence. Such lathes were used to cut circles around the ball in two directions, thereby creating a mesh pattern of lines on the surface of the ball.

FORGAN SPOON

In 1852 Robert Forgan entered the club-making business, working for the master clubmaker Hugh Philp. Forgan learned the art of clubmaking so well that he ran Philp's business during the last two years of Philp's life, when Hugh was ill. After Philp's death in 1856, Forgan took over the business, but under his own name. In 1863 Forgan was appointed "Golf Club Maker to H.R.H The Prince of Wales." This circa 1865 long spoon is stamped with the Prince of Wales plume and Forgan's name in large block letters. Sometime around 1870, Forgan began marking his clubs with smaller block letters.

WILSON TRACK IRON

Located in St. Andrews, Willie Wilson began making golf clubs during the late 1860s and continued into the 1890s. This circa 1870 track iron was once part of the 56 clubs collected by Harry B. Wood, author of *Golfing Curios and The Like*. Wood's book, printed in 1910, was the first book on golf collectibles ever published. This club still bears Wood's tag and is featured in his book as club number 7 in plate VI.

TRACK IRON

This circa 1850s track iron is typical for its era. The blade is thick, gracefully dished, incredibly small, and nearly round in profile. The hosel is thick, 5 1/2 inches long, and very heavy. All these characteristics are evidence of an early, well-made track iron.

GREIG LONG SPOON

Alexander Greig was a fine golfer. On New Years Day of 1851, Greig defeated no less than Tom Morris, winning his ball. As a clubmaker, Greig was also talented. He worked independently for brief periods, but when his life came to an unfortunate end (he was found drowned on the shore) Greig was employed by Jack Morris, at Royal Liverpool. This long spoon dates to the 1860s.

FORGAN PUTTER

In 1856 when Robert Forgan first began making his own clubs, he stamped them "R. Forgan" in large block letters. In 1863 Forgan began to include the Prince of Wales plume or three-feather crest, the result of being appointed clubmaker to H.R.H. The Prince of Wales. This putter dates before 1863, as the head is marked with only Forgan's large letter stamp.

MORRIS SHORT SPOON

Only a few early golfers played left-handed. As late as 1898, a commentary in *Golf* stated that a left-handed professional had never been heard of, and should one enter the Open Championship, his appearance would create as great a sensation in the world of golf as that caused by a bearded lady or dog-faced man in the outside world. This unused Tom Morris short spoon was made expressly for SWM Michael and has his name written in ink on the sole. Over the years, a number of Morris clubs have sold at auction, his earliest examples having brought prices as high as $15,000.

GRAY TRACK IRON

In 1851 both Tom Morris and John Gray became founding members of the Prestwick Golf Club and the Prestwick Mechanics Club (renamed Prestwick St. Nicholas Golf Club in 1858). At the time, Gray, an avid golfer, was a local blacksmith working with his father at a horseshoe forge. The creation of these two organizations prompted Gray to begin forging iron clubheads as part of his business.

ROBERTSON LONG SPOON

Born in 1815, Allan Robertson was the
finest golfer of his day until his death in
1859. He worked as a ballmaker in St.
Andrews, as ball making was, indeed, his
primary business. However, he also made
a few clubs. On no less than two separate
occasions, Tom Morris acknowledged that
he learned to make both clubs and balls
from Robertson to whom he was appren-
ticed and for whom he worked until their
parting in 1848. This Robertson club is
the property of the USGA.

A. FORGAN DRIVING PUTTER

Born in 1846, Andrew Forgan worked as an
apprentice to his brother, Robert Forgan, in
the early 1860s and continued making clubs
into the early 1900s. Andrew was a superb
clubmaker, as can be seen in the graceful
lines of this circa 1870 driving putter;
however, he was not as prolific as his
brother. Instead of setting up a clubmaking
business and employing a few hands, he
worked many years as a greenkeeper and
made clubs to supplement his income.

DAVIDSON SPOON

Born in 1801, Robert Davidson made clubs during the feather ball era and into the gutty ball era. He marked his clubs, including this circa 1860 short spoon, with his name in script. The elongated shape of this clubhead (all long nose clubs for that matter) required the golfer to swing with a greater emphasis on timing than on speed. Early golfers were strong enough, but they seldom, if ever, applied all their strength to their downswing. To do so almost guaranteed that the toe of the club would be open at impact. Long drivers during this era were invariably wild drivers.

PARK BRASSEY SPOON

This circa 1860s Willie Park brassey spoon has a brass plate covering the entire sole. Installing such a plate made the club more durable. Only a few long nose clubs were made with brass soleplates. With the advent of the bulger in 1890, brass sole-plates came into their own. Thereafter, the "brassey," a lofted wood shod with a brass plate, was routinely found in players' bags.

PARK PUTTER

Born in 1833, Willie Park has the distinct honor of being the first Open champion in the history of golf. Winning in 1860, Park went on to win the British Open three more times, in 1863, 1866, and 1875. To "Auld Willie," as he was affectionately known, there was no such thing as a friendly match. It was either death or glory. To his greatest friend, he was the deadliest enemy while the match lasted. Park crafted this putter around 1870.

AULD PAWKIE

This putter was made, owned, and used by Willie Park. It was presented to the Woking Golf Club 1930, and the shaft bears a sterling plaque which reads, "This putter 'AULD PAWKIE' was used by Willie Park Snr. Musselburgh in the championship of 1863, and is presented to J. Stewart Paton Esqre. of Woking Golf Club by Herbert Caldwell, 1930 'IT HOLED MANY A GUID PUTT!'" Woking sold this club at auction in 1996 for $60,000.

SANDISON PUTTER

Working in Aberdeen, Scotland, Ludovic Sandison followed in the footsteps of Alex Munro, Aberdeen's resident clubmaker prior to his death in 1847. Sandison made both fishing rods and golf clubs. He stamped both his name and his location on his clubs. Today, his clubs are scarce indeed. This Sandison putter sold at a Phillips auction in 1990 for $10,000.

DUNN PUTTER

Hailing from Musselburgh, Willie Dunn and his twin brother Jamie were born in 1821, the same year as Tom Morris. Like Morris, Willie Dunn was both a fine clubmaker and a talented golfer. Recalling Willie's swing, one of his contemporaries described it as grand and majestic, noting that on Dunn's tee-shots you wondered when his ball was going to stop!

LOFTING IRON

This circa 1860 iron is shaped like the heavy irons used in the feather ball era. It has a well-dished face and sharp saw-tooth nicking atop the hosel. It is not, however, as large or as heavy as its earlier brothers, and it is more refined in form. This club was once part of Harry B. Wood's collection and bears his tag.

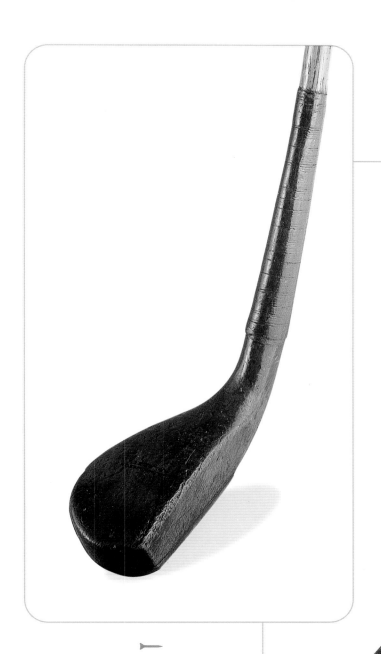

MORRIS LONG SPOON

The Grand Old Man of Golf, Tom Morris was more than a gifted clubmaker, a talented player, and a respected professional—he epitomized the game. He received accolades of all kinds but he remained a kind, honest, respectful, and humble man. Because of his character and reputation, Old Tom changed the public perception of a professional golfer from that of a rogue without a real occupation to someone worthy of society's respect. This early 1850s Tom Morris long spoon has a long, shallow face and slender neck, much like the clubs made by Hugh Philp.

DUNN SHORT SPOON

In 1851, Willie Dunn was appointed keeper of the green at Blackheath (London). He remained there for 13 years. In 1865 he returned to Leith where he was clubmaker, ball maker, and custodian to the Leith Thistle Golf Club. In 1870 he moved to Musselburgh and remained there until his death in 1878. This short spoon dates to Dunn's early days at Blackheath.

WALKER PLAY CLUB

Jack Walker worked as a clubmaker in Aberdeen during the 1860s before going to work for Willie Park around 1870. While working on his own in Aberdeen, he taught club and ball making to Robert Ferguson, who, years later, won three British Open championships in a row. .

MCEWAN PLAY CLUB

This play club consists of an unused McEwan clubhead circa 1865 and an Anderson & Sons fishing rod shaft circa 1892. The club was probably assembled by Anderson. Using such a handsome long nose clubhead to display this beautiful shaft is certainly understandable.

CLEEK

Allan Robertson is credited as the first to use an iron—a cleek—to approach the green. This was in 1848. Cleeks, as a specific type of iron, evolved from the earlier light iron, but they were neither as large nor as heavy as a light iron. They offered greater control and utility. Cleeks have a long, shallow blade with little loft, and the topline runs nearly parallel to the sole. By 1875, cleeks were in wide use. This circa 1850s cleek, formerly part of the Harry B. Wood collection, even has a distinct hook to the face like many a long nose wood.

WILSON PUTTER

James Wilson worked for Hugh Philp for 23 years. In 1852, the same year that Philp hired Robert Forgan, Wilson started his own clubmaking business, opening a shop in St. Andrews. After Philp's death, Wilson and Forgan became friendly rivals. Often they purchased their wood together. After dividing it, they would draw lots to determine who would get what.

MCEWAN BAFFING SPOON

Having the shortest shaft in the spoon family, baffy spoons also have the most loft. Prior to the 1850s, baffys were used to approach the green from close distance. Irons were used primarily when the ball lay in trouble, and the golfer did not want to risk damaging a wooden head. During the 1850s, however, a few golfers began to use a cleek (iron) to approach the green, thereby displacing the baffy. This McEwan baffy dates to the 1850s.

Clubmakers continued to make long nose woods throughout this period. Perhaps the most significant was Thomas Johnston's vulcanite club. Johnston's club, designed to be more durable than wooden clubs, was not a commercial success—far from it. The fact that Johnston patented his club in 1876, however, marks it as a milestone in golf. Johnston's is the first golf club, of literally thousands, ever to be patented. ◦ As long nose woods continued to evolve, they were made with deeper faces and thicker necks. During the late 1880s, a fair number were made with a distinctly shorter head. Today such clubs are referred to as "transitionals." Born because of the continual damage inflicted to the club head by the unyielding gutty ball, transitionals reflect the natural trend toward shortening the head to make it more durable. Starting out as a small stylistic change, the transitional quickly evolved into the bulger which, devised in 1888, overtook the market in the 1890s (see page 60). ◦ True transitional clubheads, providing the transition between the end of the long nose and the acceptance of the bulger, were made in a variety of shapes and head lengths. Some are "semi-long nose" while others are much shorter than a long nose clubhead but still longer than the common bulger. Transitionals look out of proportion when compared to the overall profile of a long nose clubhead, nor do they have the long, graceful lines of a long nose. ◦ Irons made during this time continued to get smaller and take on an expanded role. Once used only when the ball was in trouble, irons were used more and more when approaching the green. By 1890 the track iron, with its thick, tiny head, had been replaced by the niblick, with its lighter and distinctly larger head which made it easier to use from a normal lie. The mashie, invented around 1880, filled the perceived gap between the lofter and the niblick. In 1889 Willie Park Jr. received a patent—the second ever issued for a golf club and the first ever issued for an iron—for his concave face lofter, yet another new iron club. ◦ As the game began to spread, more clubmakers came into existence. Clubmakers had definite standards (becoming a clubmaker required serving up to 4 years or longer as an apprentice) and lived by their reputations. Everything they did to a club was done with a purpose in mind—from where the wood pegs were placed in the horn, to the face depth, head width, and neck size. Clubs were well-measured and carefully crafted entirely by hand. The better clubmakers shaped their clubs with just a touch more grace and style; the head was balanced in design and its profile appealed to the eye. ◦ The golf balls in use between 1870 and 1890 were solid gutta percha. Most were formed in molds having a smooth interior then placed in a specially devised lathe that cut lines into the ball. After one set of lines encircled the ball, the ball was turned 90 degrees on axis and the second set of lines was cut. One can usually recognize a line-cut ball by the asymmetry of the lines and/or the varying sizes and depths of the lines.

MANZIE GRASSED DRIVER

Thomas Manzie is best remembered as the professional who, in 1876, succeeded Bob Kirk at Royal Blackheath. He worked there until 1885. This circa 1880 Manzie is termed a grassed driver. It is as long as a regular play club but has just a little more loft, so the club could be used through the green, given an appropriate lie.

CARRICK CLEEK

Sometime in the late 1850s or early 1860s, Francis Carrick and Archibald Carrick Jr. took over the blacksmith/tool manufacturing business of their fathers. For F.&A. Carrick, forging clubheads was a sideline to their primary business of making hand tools. The known Carrick irons usually date to the 1880s or earlier. They are usually marked "X" along with "Carrick" or "F.&A. Carrick," and some, like this circa 1880 cleek, are also marked "Musselburgh."

T. DUNN PLAY CLUB

Tom Dunn, son of Willie Dunn Sr. and brother of Willie Dunn Jr., learned the art of clubmaking from his father before starting his own business at North Berwick in 1870. In the autumn of that year, Dunn accepted the position of professional to the London Scottish Golf Club in Wimbledon. He remained there until 1881 when he accepted the duties of custodian of the links at North Berwick, a position he held until 1889. Tom Dunn was also a prolific golf course designer, laying out 137 courses.

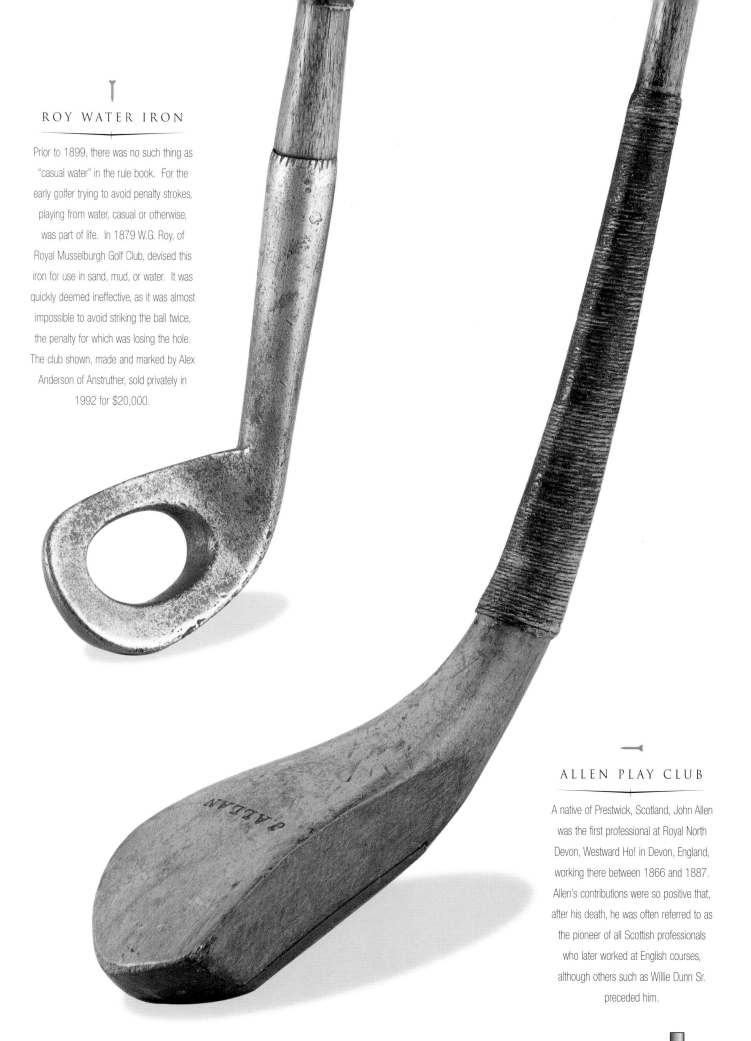

ROY WATER IRON

Prior to 1899, there was no such thing as "casual water" in the rule book. For the early golfer trying to avoid penalty strokes, playing from water, casual or otherwise, was part of life. In 1879 W.G. Roy, of Royal Musselburgh Golf Club, devised this iron for use in sand, mud, or water. It was quickly deemed ineffective, as it was almost impossible to avoid striking the ball twice, the penalty for which was losing the hole. The club shown, made and marked by Alex Anderson of Anstruther, sold privately in 1992 for $20,000.

ALLEN PLAY CLUB

A native of Prestwick, Scotland, John Allen was the first professional at Royal North Devon, Westward Ho! in Devon, England, working there between 1866 and 1887. Allen's contributions were so positive that, after his death, he was often referred to as the pioneer of all Scottish professionals who later worked at English courses, although others such as Willie Dunn Sr. preceded him.

HUNTER LONG SPOON

Charlie Hunter was Prestwick's custodian of the links from 1864 to 1921, except for a brief stint, from the middle of 1865 to 1868, when he worked at Blackheath. He learned clubmaking from Tom Morris who worked at Prestwick from 1851 to 1864. Like Tom Morris, Hunter was well-loved by those who knew him and was referred to in print as "the Grand Old Man of the West."

MORRIS PLAY CLUB

Tom Morris won the British Open in 1861, '62, '64, '67. His son, Tom Jr., also won the Open four times, in 1868, '69, '70, and '72. Young Tom, who became a partner in his father's clubmaking business in 1869, died in 1875 at age 24. Old Tom, the professional and keeper of the green at the Royal and Ancient Golf Club between 1864 and 1904, died in 1908 at age 87.

FERGUSON SHORT SPOON

Born in 1848, Robert Ferguson won the
British Open three years in a row: 1880,
'81, '82. He was a gifted clubmaker, but
clubmaking was never his primary focus.
To him, the game was the thing. With the
decline of his play, Ferguson spent more of
his time as a coach and caddie than he did
as a clubmaker. During the final 20 years
of his life he was relegated to working as a
caddie, oftentimes prosecuted by the local
justices for failure to apply for a caddie
license. Ferguson died in 1915. This
short spoon sold privately in
1988 for $4,500.

WILSON LOFTER

According to 1893 Open champion Willie
Auchterlonie, Robert Wilson was the first
man to make iron clubheads in St. Andrews.
While there can be no doubt that St.
Andrews had its share of blacksmiths
who pounded out a few iron heads even
centuries prior to Wilson, Wilson was most
likely the first to produce iron clubheads
in significant quantities.

J. MORRIS GRASSED DRIVER

Born in 1847, Jack Morris was the son of George Morris, Old Tom's brother. In 1869, Jack went to work at Hoylake and remained there as the professional until 1929. Jack did not make nearly as many clubs as his uncle, Tom Morris, nor were Jack's clubs as well made or attractive.

HUTCHISON SPOON

Born in 1847, James Hutchison was a fine clubmaker located at North Berwick from the 1880s to the early 1900s. This Hutchison long spoon dates to the early 1880s, but has an exceptional shape and style not often found in clubs made during this time.

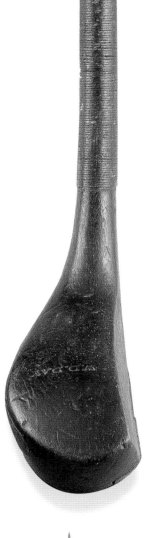

DAY WOODEN NIBLICK

Born in 1837, Walter Day worked as a clubmaker during the second half of the 19th century. This wooden niblick looks much like a long nose club, except that the head is significantly smaller and has a full metal soleplate. Such clubs were designed to drive a ball from amongst stones or out of a rut that would allow the smaller head.

This circa 1880 John Gray cleek was the equivalent of today's long iron. It was designed to loft the ball, at no great height, and allow it to run along the fairway up to the hole. It was also very useful for approaching in the teeth of a wind.

STRATH PUTTER

Born in 1850, David Strath was the beloved friend and golfing companion of young Tom Morris. In 1876, Strath tied for the Open championship at St. Andrews, but refused to play off. The last day, aided by a strong following wind, he hit his ball onto the 17th green before the group ahead had holed out. His ball was stopped by a rub of the green, but a player insisted that Strath be disqualified for hitting into the group ahead. After completing his round, Strath was told the tie would be played-off under protest. Strath refused to play unless the committee cleared his name first. With Strath's refusal, the committee awarded the title to Bob Martin. Like young Tom, David Strath did not reach the age of 30.

M. PARK SHORT SPOON

Born in 1839, Mungo Park was the brother of Willie Park. He was a seafarer for much of his early life, but he did win the British Open in 1874, defeating none other than young Tom Morris by two shots. His first round of 75 was nothing short of phenomenal, approached only in the second round by young Tom's 78 and Bob Martin's 79. No other competitor scored below 80 in either round. This circa 1880s spoon, with its deeper face, sold privately in 2001 for $8,500.

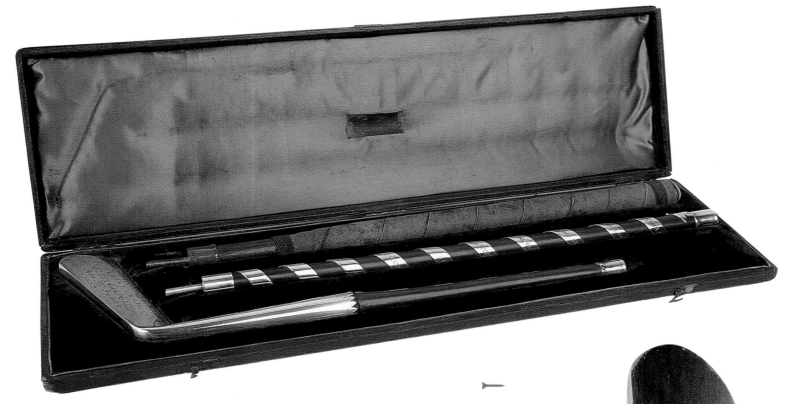

EDINBURGH CLEEK CLUB

Members of the Edinburgh Cleek Golf Club competed for this 3-piece trophy club which dates to 1887. The head is sterling silver, and the middle section of the wood shaft is wrapped with sterling silver. The grip is sheepskin. This club is on display at USGA Golf House.

MITCHELL PUTTER

David Mitchell was a clubmaker at St. Andrews in the early 1870s. In 1876 he replaced Frank Bell as the clubmaker at Carnoustie. Little else is known about Mitchell, who died in 1883. His clubs are graceful and attractive, but few remain.

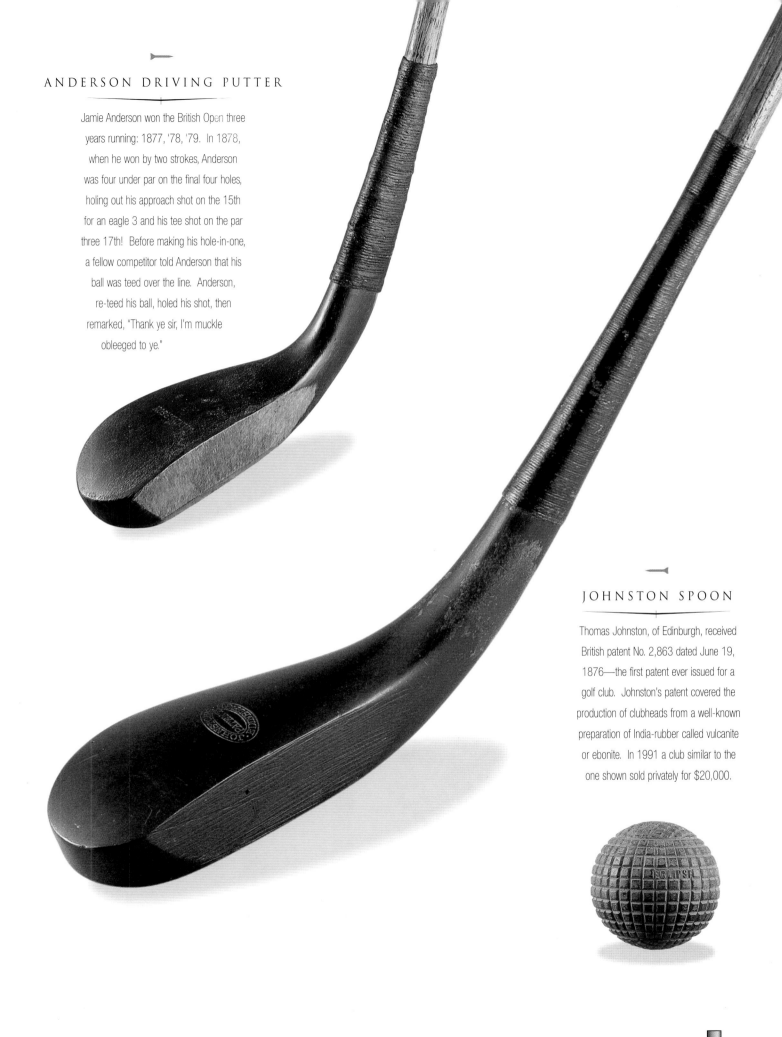

ANDERSON DRIVING PUTTER

Jamie Anderson won the British Open three years running: 1877, '78, '79. In 1878, when he won by two strokes, Anderson was four under par on the final four holes, holing out his approach shot on the 15th for an eagle 3 and his tee shot on the par three 17th! Before making his hole-in-one, a fellow competitor told Anderson that his ball was teed over the line. Anderson, re-teed his ball, holed his shot, then remarked, "Thank ye sir, I'm muckle obleeged to ye."

JOHNSTON SPOON

Thomas Johnston, of Edinburgh, received British patent No. 2,863 dated June 19, 1876—the first patent ever issued for a golf club. Johnston's patent covered the production of clubheads from a well-known preparation of India-rubber called vulcanite or ebonite. In 1991 a club similar to the one shown sold privately for $20,000.

ANDERSON JR. PLAY CLUB

David Anderson Jr. was the son of a well-known St. Andrews personality nicknamed "Old Da," and the brother of three time British Open champion Jamie Anderson. The clubs marked "D. Anderson" were usually made by Junior, his father being better known as a ballmaker, greenkeeper, and caddie. This circa 1885 Anderson play club has a fishing rod shaft somewhat similar to the one shown on page 46.

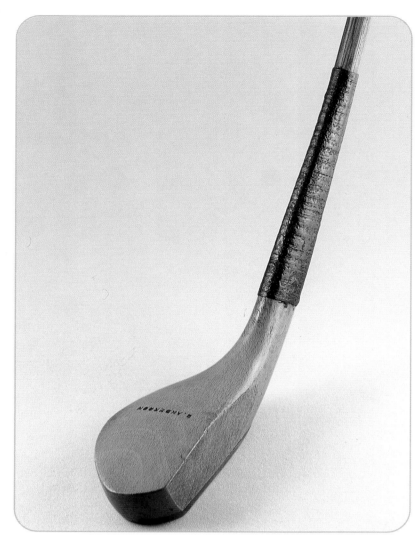

WILSON MASHIE

Introduced by 1881, the mashie grew in popularity and, by the early 1890s, became a mainstay of the golfer's arsenal. Originally, mashies were a cross between a lofter and a niblick, the blade being a little shorter and taller than a lofter's. This Willie Wilson gunmetal mashie, sold by the Army & Navy Co-Operative Society Ltd., dates to the 1880s. Note the "M" for mashie.

MORRIS PLAY CLUB

This circa 1880 Tom Morris play club is the oldest known club to use steel in its shaft. The shaft is actually made from 12 length-wise pieces of cane—six inner and six outer—around a tubular steel core which is visible at the end of the shaft. The shaft was probably made by Hardy Brothers of Alnwick, England, or Fosters of Ashborn, England, and is similar to those they made as fishing rods at the same time.

PARK JR. SHORT SPOON

Willie Park Jr. won the British Open in 1887 and 1889. This circa late 1880s short spoon has a head that is shorter and thicker than the traditional long nose, yet is longer and sleeker than the bulger, shown below. Today, such intermediate clubs are termed transitionals.

FORGAN BULGER

In 1888 Henry Lamb introduced his "bulger" driver to a group of professionals, and then to the world. At the time, it was a radical design. The head was much shorter and broader than a long nose, and the traditional concave face of the long nose wood was not only eliminated, it was reversed! The bulging face is clearly discernable on this circa 1890 Robert Forgan driver.

Between 1890 and 1900, the world of golf began to expand as never before. In 1889 there were 290 golf clubs in the UK; by 1900 the number had grown to 1,357. The oldest permanent golf club in the United States, the St. Andrews Golf Club at Yonkers-on Hudson, New York, was established in November of 1888. By January 1, 1899, there were 750 clubs in America and over 200,000 players. During this period, golf began to take hold in other countries such as Canada, Australia, France, and South Africa. No longer was golf an obscure game played by a small number of hardy souls over the links of Scotland and England. • Prior to 1890, long nose woods were the norm. After 1890 they were quickly replaced by the "bulger." Invented by Henry Lamb in 1888, bulger woods had shorter, broader heads, and their faces bulged outward towards the target. These were radical changes. The traditional concave face inherent in the long nose wood was not only eliminated, it was reversed. Lamb believed that a convex face would minimize hooking and slicing, especially for shots struck on the heel or the toe of the wood. Another reason for abandoning the length and shape of the long nose head was to put more clubhead mass directly behind the ball and to make the club more durable. • Henry Lamb coined the name "bulger," began using the club himself, and presented it to a group of professionals for their inspection. It continues in use today. Truly, Lamb's creation stands as one of the most important and longest lasting innovations in golf equipment. • Between 1890 and 1900, irons became more refined and more plentiful. Golfers now carried more irons than woods, as the use of irons to approach the green became the standard. New kinds of irons appeared on the scene, everything from the "glory" iron to the "sky" iron, from the spade niblick to the bar back cleek. • Just as the bulger replaced the long nose wood, the blade putter (putting cleek) replaced the long nose putter. This was a reversal of the general consensus, held prior to 1890, that blade putters were ineffective and undesirable. The new putters were made from either gunmetal or iron. • During this era of dramatic growth, clubmakers began to experiment with clubs that incorporated a fascinating array of ideas, designs, and materials. Aiding the golfer was not the clubmaker's only motivation for coming up with a new design. The other goal was market share. If a clubmaker or inventor designed a unique club that became widely accepted, his or her idea could be profitable. Consequently, during the 1890s a number of clubs were patented. Most, however, proved unprofitable. • The golf ball continued to be made from gutta percha and in a variety of styles. Most were formed in molds that had the ball markings or a series of raised concentric rings formed inside. No longer were cutting lathes needed to mark the ball, though some remained in use. In 1899 the "Haskell" golf ball, made from wound elastic thread enclosed inside a gutta percha cover, was patented in the U.S. by Coburn Haskell and Bertram Work. In a few short years the Haskell, or "Bounding Billy" as it was sometimes called, would render the gutta percha ball obsolete.

Resembling a sledgehammer more than a golf club, Captain Hamilton's The Pendulum putter was modeled after a croquet mallet. The teak wood head measures 2 3/4 inches in face depth and 4 1/2 inches in length. In 1891, this putter was reviewed in *Golf* and recommended only to those who suffer from vertigo, headaches, or confused vision when "stooping" to putt —and to women!

CURRIE METALWOOD

William Currie Jr., an india rubber manufacturer in Edinburgh, Scotland, received the first patent ever issued for a metalwood—a British patent (No. 5741) dated April 3, 1891. The head of Currie's club is made from gunmetal and is filled with red gutta percha exposed at the face. Gutta percha was the same material used to make golf balls during Currie's day.

THE SKIBBIE

Charles Ashford received a British patent dated November 10, 1893, that covered a clubhead made from both wood and iron. The neck and entire bottom of Ashford's "Skibbie" are formed from a single piece of metal. Ashford sought to combine the durability of an iron club with the driving power of a wooden club.

CRESCENT IRON

Known during its brief day as a Crescent iron, this club was covered under Robert Ramsbottom's British patent dated August 2, 1894. Ramsbottom calculated that the claw hosel would make a tighter joint and reduce shaft breakage. In 1992 this Crescent iron sold privately for $4,500.

JOHNSON BRASSEY

Walter Claude Johnson received a British patent dated May 4, 1893, that covered his unique brassey. Remove the three screws in the brass disc atop the head and the disc comes off. Weight can then be added or removed. The shaft is held in place by a brass ferrule, not a traditional neck. The golfer had only to unscrew a single screw to remove a broken shaft. Unfortunately, the ferrule actually made the shaft more likely to break.

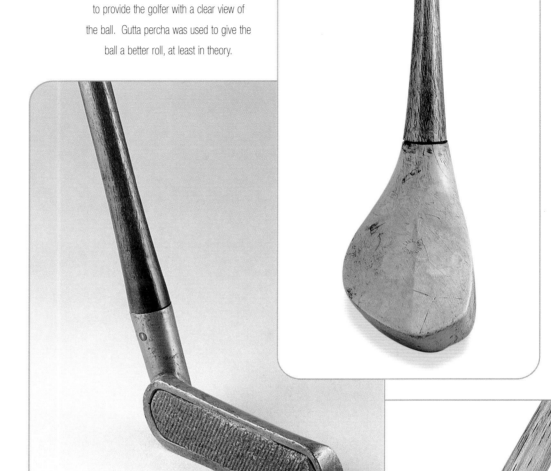

CELLULOID DRIVER

Robert Brand, of the North British Rubber Co., received a British patent dated June 11, 1890, for this celluloid head driver. Later that year, *Golf* slyly recommended a celluloid club "to a man against whom you are going to play a match for money."

ALLAWAY PUTTER

Devised by W. Allaway of A.&D. Padon, Edinburgh, the Allaway putter has a gun-metal head inlaid with red gutta percha. The face is set ahead of the shaft in order to provide the golfer with a clear view of the ball. Gutta percha was used to give the ball a better roll, at least in theory.

ACME PUTTER

In 1896 George Forrester received a British registered design that covered his Acme putter. Forrester thought his club, with its deep face and overhanging flange, would aid alignment. When using this club to address the ball, the golfer cannot see the edge of the sole, and the back of the ball appears flat.

HODGKIN DRIVER

This driver has an iron frame, completely open on all sides except for the socket, filled with a wood block. Six screws extend through the head, top to bottom, to fasten the block to the frame. The face is covered with leather to protect the wood from damage. In 1893 John Hodgkin received a British patent for this club.

SWENY DRIVER

Marked "Sweny Patent Albany, NY" on the head, this driver was covered under a US patent issued to Henry Sweny on August 18, 1896. The neck rises from the top of the head to position the shaft on axis with the center of a deep face. A similar Sweny driver sold at a January 1996 Phillips auction in England for $5,500.

SPALDING DUPLEX

Dating to the late 1890s, this putter/utility club is marked "The Spalding, Hand Forged." One side of the head has a little more loft than the other. This club can be used as a putter either croquet style or in a traditional manner, right- or left-handed. It can also be used for right- or left-handed trouble shots.

SWENY DRIVER

This crosshead driver is marked "H.R. Sweny / SPT'G Goods Co." on the shaft. Henry Roy Sweny, of Albany, New York, operated a sporting goods store while creating a few clubs of his own design during the middle 1890s. In 1899, he sold his fledgling Golf Goods Manufactuing Company. An unmarked Sweny crosshead driver sold at the 1994 Sporting Antiquities auction near Boston for $5,500.

NICOLL CLEEK

In 1893 George Nicoll applied for a British patent on his leather face iron. A patent, however, was never issued. Nicoll continued to make his cleeks, with either a leather or gutta percha face, and mark them with the patent number obtained with his application. A Nicoll leather face iron sold at the 1991 Sporting Antiquities auction for $3,300.

VESEY METALWOODS

In 1894 Thomas Vesey received a British patent that covered the metalwoods shown. Both clubs have gutta percha faces, which, according to the patent, can be repaired or replaced should they become damaged. The club on the left is made from aluminum; the club on the right is made from steel.

TWIST "T" PUTTER

Designed by George F. Twist, this putter can be used either right- or left-handed and can be adjusted to any desired lie. The golfer needed only to loosen the nut on the back of the head, adjust the blade, then retighten the nut. Twist received a British patent dated April 27, 1891. This patent is the first ever to deal with a mechanical golf club of any type.

"SC" ANTISHANK IRON

Designed to prevent the golfer from "piping" (shanking) an approach shot, the neck on this club was designed by George F. Smith, a famous Lancashire amateur. In 1897 Smith applied for a British patent to cover his design but never completed his application. Nevertheless, thousands of antishank irons were marked with Smith's name. The blade shape shown is unique.

ALEXANDER DUPLEX

Duplex woods, woods that have two faces, were made in two styles. One style provides one face for right-handed use and the other face for left-handed use. The other style provides for the use of either striking face when playing right-handed. This circa 1890 G. Alexander duplex wood shown is usable only right-handed.

MONTGOMERY PUTTER

James Colin Montgomery, of Southsea, England, received a British patent dated March 21, 1894, that covered this roller putter. According to a *Golf* review, "By means of the roller the putter cannot catch the turf and thus cause a foozle." A Montgomery roller putter sold privately in 1994 for $5,000.

BRAND PUTTER

In 1892 Willie Park Jr. began producing his wry-neck putter, the lower neck curving back to offset the blade. A radical idea when introduced, the offset blade became one of the most popular developments in the game. The circa 1895 putter shown, crafted by Charles Brand of Carnoustie, is one of a kind. It is the only wooden long nose style club ever made with a wry-neck.

URQUART ADJUSTABLE

Receiving four British patents between 1892 and 1902, Robert L. Urquhart sought the perfect adjustable iron. The example shown, covered under his November 1, 1895 British patent is simple to operate: push in the lever on the hosel, pull out the spring-loaded blade a short distance, rotate the blade to the desired loft, and fit it back in place. This club was purchased privately in 1992 for $8,000.

ANDERSON IRONS & PUTTER

In 1892 Robert Anderson, of Edinburgh, received a British patent that covered the center-shafted irons and putter shown above. Anderson believed that his club-head would be more accurate, less likely to turn on off-center hits, and more powerful, because of the weight concentrated near the end of the shaft.

A. FORGAN PUTTER

While working in Glasgow between 1893 and 1897, Andrew Forgan produced this unusual putter. The clubhead is modeled after a "shinty" stick. Shinty, a field game similar to field hockey, was once popular in Scotland, especially in the Scottish highlands.

WOODFACE PUTTER

This unmarked mid 1890s putter has an extreme degree of offset, metal at the bottom of the neck that slopes back towards the golfer, and an extraordinarily (3/4 inch) thick block of wood held in place by three screws located across the back of the head.

GRANT PUTTER & MASHIE

In 1892 George Grant of Sunningdale, England, received a British patent that covered both his center-shafted putter and the mashie shown. The putter was for normal use, but, according to Grant's patent, the mashie was designed to "more easily strike balls out of difficult places."

YOUNG METALWOOD

George Young, of Leith, Scotland, received a British patent dated May 13, 1896, that covered his metalwood. Young's club has a gunmetal head that is inlaid with a wood block at the face. Two strips of horn are fastened to the top and bottom of the wood block. Should the wood become worn, it can be changed by removing two screws in the back of the head.

FORGAN PUTTER

Marked "R. Forgan and Son / St. Andrews" on its shaft, this forked hosel putter, usable either right- or left-handed, was designed to reduce clubhead torque on mis-hit putts. The fork hosel is obviously untraditional, but so is its attachment to the shaft—the tip of the shaft is not enclosed. This club was entirely hand forged and would have been difficult and time consuming to produce.

MORRIS PUTTER

It is believed that Tom Morris developed this "drain pipe" putter (forged by Tom Stewart) in the early 1890s, when he briefly produced his two other patent clubs. In 1998 a Morris drain pipe putter sold at auction in New York City for $7,000.

ADJUSTABLE IRON

The blade on this unmarked iron extends up then back down *behind* the hosel. The hosel runs through a slot atop the blade which is sandwiched between two rectangular pieces of metal shaped to fit the blade's curve. Loosening the wing nut loosens the piece that clamps down on the blade. The blade can be adjusted to four different lofts.

PRESTON DRIVER

Made by D.Y. Preston of St. Andrews, this forward face driver was once part of the David Low collection. Low, a professional from Carnoustie, lent his small collection to the British Travel Association for display in the United States during the mid-1950s. This club is pictured in the May 1955 issue of *Golf Digest*.

CRAN CLEEK

On June 8, 1897, James Cran, of Chicopee, Massachusetts, received a US design patent that covered this iron. The wood face inlay is held in place by two screws through the back of the head. A.G. Spalding & Brothers produced this club from 1897 to 1919. The iron shown, marked "Pat applied for," was one of the first.

ADAMS PUTTER

John Adams, of Morristown, New Jersey, received a US patent dated Oct. 12, 1897, that covered this croquet style putter. The head measures 6 3/4 inches in length and 1 1/2 inches in width and depth. The shaft has a sterling silver band engraved "H.V.R." located around the shaft below the grip.

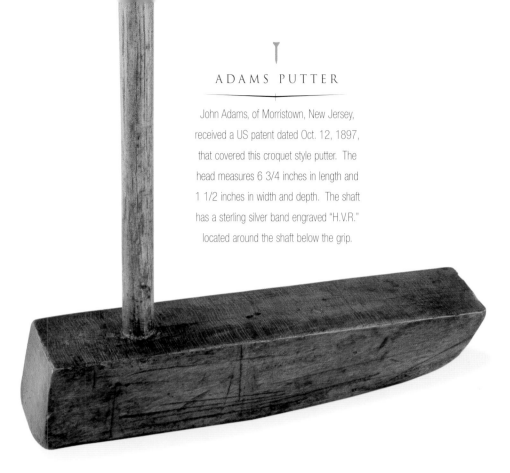

T-FRAME PUTTER

This circa 1900 T-frame putter has a number of fascinating features beyond its unique shape. The front half of the head is made from brass, while the sighting rod is made from iron. Measuring but 3/4 inches by 1/2 inch, the sole on this putter has the smallest "footprint" of any club known. The body of the head ties into the hosel halfway up its side.

BALL BACK IRON

The huge ball-shaped mound on the back of this exceptionally thick, short clubhead puts nearly all of the club's weight directly behind the ball. In theory this design makes sense; in reality, however, such concentrated weight is impractical because it leaves the golfer no room for error.

DALRYMPLE DUPLEX

Sir Walter Dalrymple, The Baronet of North Berwick, received a British patent in 1892 that covered this two-face duplex club designed to function as a mashie and a putter. When Dalrymple showed his club to Hugh Kirkaldy, the famous St. Andrews pro, Hugh remarked, "Ca' that a club? I'd sinner play wi' a tea-spin!"

INDESTRUCTIBLE WOOD

Willie Dunn Jr.'s Indestructible driver was first advertised in 1899. Dunn claimed that the short socket placed the desired spring closer to the head, that there was no horn to work loose, that elasticity was gained by using a wood block, and that the grain of the wood ran directly with the blow.

PENDULUM PUTTER

The first croquet-style putter to be patented, the Pendulum putter was covered under James Munro's British patent dated July 4, 1896. Munro's putter was made by The Scottish Golf Club Manufacturing Company, the first company ever to make clubs entirely by mechanized means.

SIMPLEX NIBLICK

Francis Brewster devised an entire set of center-shafted "crosshead" clubs, from driver to putter. His Simplex clubs met with little success even though he wrote a book and formed the Simplex Golf Association to provide instruction. Brewster's 1897 British patent covered this Simplex niblick.

FORRESTER MASHIE

William Ballingall's British patent dated January 16, 1894, was the first patent granted for a flange on either an iron or a putter. Ballingall's irons were produced with a 1/2 inch wide flange. This mid-1890s iron, made by George Forrester of Elie and Earlsferry, has a flange that measures a touch over a full inch in width.

BROUGHAM METALWOOD

Reginald Brougham received a British patent dated Nov. 20, 1893, for this aluminum driver. The wood face is actually a block of wood that is set into the head and held in place by two screws, one in the sole and one in the back of the head. By constructing an aluminum head with a wood face, Brougham was trying to combine the durability of metal with the feel of wood.

AUCHTERLONIE BRASSEY

Born in St. Andrews in 1873, Willie Auchterlonie won the 1893 British Open. Nevertheless, Auchterlonie limited his golfing exploits in order to pursue his primary interest: clubmaking. A matching putter is on display at the British Golf Museum in St. Andrews.

DUNN DRIVER

A few clubmakers tried forming the head and shaft from a single piece of wood. Most of these jointless creations were made around 1900. John Duncan Dunn received a British patent dated July 25, 1894, that covered the one-piece driver shown. It was Dunn who brought the one-piece club to prominence.

ROSS IRON

Made with a hollow bronze head and a tempered steel face held in place by three large bronze rivets, this spring-face iron was patented by William Ross. Ross's 1893 British patent was the first to cover a club with a face designed to provide a trampoline effect.

WALKER PUTTER

Devised with a piece of spring steel suspended across the face, this spring-face putter was covered under a British patent issued to George Walker, of Coventry, England, in 1895. Walker was trying to combine the elasticity of a wooden face with the durability of a metal one.

CUSHING ADJUSTABLE

By means of a thumbscrew, the loft of this club can be changed to any one of three different positions. Harry Cushing received a US patent dated November 20, 1899, that covered this adjustable iron.

SLADE METALWOOD

On July 28, 1896, Edward Slade, of Newton, Massachusetts, received the first US patent that covered a metalwood. Slade's club has a wood block set into an aluminum head. The block is backed by elastic material, and the desired spring-face effect is controlled by a screw in the rear of the head.

ANDERSON NIBLICK

Made by Anderson & Sons of Edinburgh, this early 1890s wooden niblick has a small, slender head, the bottom *half* of which is a solid, cambered piece of brass. Another example of this club sold at a 1996 Phillips auction in New York City for $7,000.

As golf's popularity continued to mushroom, clubmaking became more and more mechanized. Most club-makers used woodcutting lathes to turn out wooden heads and shafts. Most cleekmakers, those clubmakers who produced iron clubheads, made their irons by drop forging—filling a die with iron, pressing the iron into shape, then drilling out the hosel. What took clubmakers hours to fashion by hand in the 1890s could now be produced in a matter of minutes. • The booming golf market increased its use of advertising, and that changed the cosmetics of the golf club, especially those made from metal. Clubmakers began to stamp a variety of marks on their work, such as their name and location, the name and location of the seller, and other promotional statements such as "Made in Scotland" and "Warranted Hand Forged." Trademarks were used by many cleekmakers and became more graphic, including bees, snakes, flowers, mountains, guns, arrows, birds, and hundreds of others. • By 1904 the socket neck wood, introduced and patented in 1891 by Robert Anderson of Edinburgh, Scotland, had overtaken the centuries-old splice neck as the primary method used to join wooden heads to wood shafts. Splice necks were formed by cutting the neck at an angle, cutting the shaft at a corresponding angle, and then gluing and whipping them together with pitched twine. The socket neck was formed by drilling a hole down the neck then inserting the shaft. • Face scoring on irons, tried as far back as 1873, came of age. Lines and dot punches in a variety of patterns were widely used. Some makers, however, continued to offer smooth face irons. • Clubmakers continued to try innovative designs, though most were quickly rejected. Of all the new clubs devised during this period, the Schenectady putter was the most historic. Patented in 1903 by Arthur Knight of Schenectady, New York, the Schenectady putter was deftly used by the short-hitting Walter Travis when he defeated the long-hitting Edward "Ted" Blackwell in the 1904 British Amateur Championship. Those living in the UK did not take kindly to seeing their championship won for the first time by a foreigner, and they quickly identified Travis's unorthodox putter as having given him an unfair advantage. • In 1910 the R&A finally ruled the Schenectady and all other center-shafted putters to be illegal, much to the chagrin of the USGA which declined to outlaw the Schenectady. The resulting controversy over the legality of the Schenectady threatened the amicable working relationship between the USGA and the R&A. Such a break might have resulted in allowing the game to evolve in two different and incompatible directions. Fortunately, the governing bodies did not let their differences over the Schenectady diminish their desire to work together. It was 1951, however, before the R&A lifted their ban against the Schenectady and other center-shafted putters. • By 1905 the Haskell rubber core ball, invented in 1899, had completely replaced the gutty ball. Most golfers found they could hit a Haskell farther than any gutta percha ball. In the years following its introduction, the rubber core ball underwent continual change. Innumerable variations in both surface pattern and composition of the ball were tried. While the basic idea of winding vulcanized elastic around a core did not change, manufacturers experimented with a wide variety of core materials.

ARLINGTON PUTTER

Produced in 1906 by the Columbus Brass Company, of Columbus, Ohio, the Arlington Putter has a cylindrical brass head that is usable both left- and right-handed. The clubhead consists of three separate threaded pieces that screw together.

DOLPHIN DRIVER

The streamline design of the Dolphin driver not only reduced wind resistance, it also concentrated as much clubhead mass as possible directly behind the ball. As was true of many abandoned clubs, the Dolphin driver sounded good in theory but proved impractical in actual play.

SPRAGUE PUTTER

Patented in the US in 1904 by William W. Davis and marked "G.S. Sprague and Co. Boston," this putter has four striking faces and the hosel/shaft can be moved to any desired position. To adjust the shaft, one simply holds the head firmly in one hand while turning the hosel with the other hand. When the ball joint loosens, the shaft will swivel in any direction. Select the new position, and lock the shaft in place by turning the hosel in the opposite direction.

DUAL FACE IRON

The designers thought that the lower section of the face would pass under the ball giving the ball the necessary loft to lift it out of the rough or sand. The upper section, which has considerably less loft, would then contact the ball and give it distance not possible with an ordinary lofting club. This early 1900s gunmetal iron is marked with the names of Ashley Davey and F. Hopper, two British professionals.

CENTRO IRON

John C. L. Henry, of Glasgow, received a British patent dated July 13, 1904, for this iron. Henry believed his centershafted clubs would hit straighter shots by reducing the torque at impact. A Centro iron sold for $6,000 at the July 2001 Phillips golf auction held in Chester, England.

CROSSHEAD PUTTER

This unmarked putter is shaped more like a shark's tooth than a golf club! Such centershafted clubs became illegal in the UK in 1910. Note the circular lead weight inlaid in the center of the fiber face insert. It was thought that lead, being a soft metal, would give the golfer greater "feel." The idea never caught on because lead is easily dented.

MURRAY PUTTER

The head of this putter is made from gunmetal inlaid with wood across the top. The sole and greenheart shaft are stamped "D. Murray, Brechin." Fashioned on the same center shaft principle as the Schenectady putter, Murray's putter dates prior to 1910, when the R&A ruled that center shaft mallet putters were illegal.

SLAZENGER PUTTER

Produced by F.L. Slazenger & Co., New York, this triangle head putter was reviewed in the UK in a 1903 issue of *Golfing*. The complaint was made that the back of the head was apt to catch on the ground if a normal putting stroke was used.

FORGAN MASHIE

This perforated face mashie was designed for use around water. In the early 1900s the golfer did not receive relief when in casual water in a bunker or other hazard, nor from ditches and streams, etc. This Forgan iron is marked with the king's crown stamp used by Forgan between 1902 and 1910.

ADJUSTABLE IRON

The blade on this adjustable iron can rotate 360 degrees. Its unique shape allows the blade to look and perform the same way for either left- or right-handed golfers. The shape and thinness of the blade, however, made it difficult to hit the ball solidly.

GARNER PUTTER

The Garner putter was designed not only for both left- and right-handed use, it was also designed to function like a billiard cue. As pictured, the putter is resting on the sides of its disc-shaped faces. This allows the sole, which is perfectly flat, to become the active striking face—in billiard cue fashion. One month after John Garner applied for a patent in 1904, the R&A outlawed using a golf club "in the same manner as a billiard ball is struck with a cue." This club sold at a 1988 Phillips golf auction in New York City for $3300.

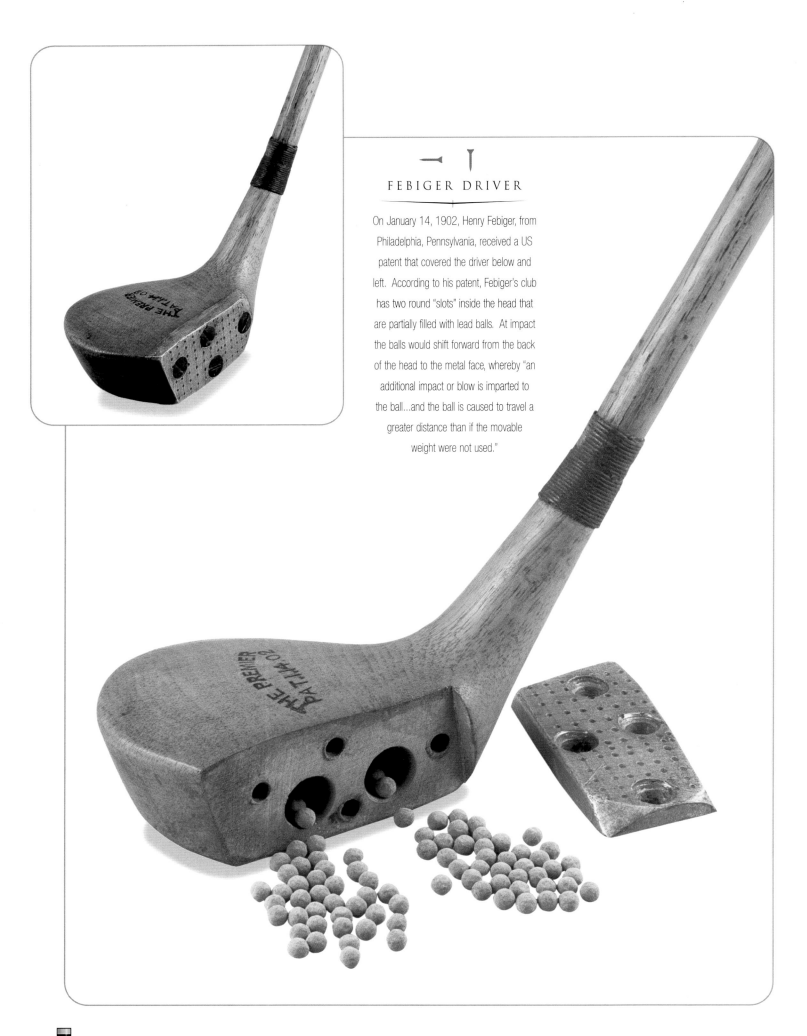

FEBIGER DRIVER

On January 14, 1902, Henry Febiger, from Philadelphia, Pennsylvania, received a US patent that covered the driver below and left. According to his patent, Febiger's club has two round "slots" inside the head that are partially filled with lead balls. At impact the balls would shift forward from the back of the head to the metal face, whereby "an additional impact or blow is imparted to the ball...and the ball is caused to travel a greater distance than if the movable weight were not used."

TAYLOR MASHIE

According to Frederick Taylor's US patent issued June 30, 1903, the goal of his design was to increase the backspin. To accomplish this, the faces of his baffies, mashies, mid-irons, and niblicks were to have "outwardly-projecting teeth, which by preference [are] of the kind usually formed upon the file-cut portion of a rasp." Taylor's patent, however, does not comment on what the ball would look like after the shot.

HARDINGHAM PUTTER

In December of 1905 Arthur Hardingham received a British patent that covered his T-frame putter, designed to aid alignment. To prevent the long alignment bar from scuffing the ground during the golfer's stroke, the rear of the sole rounds up.

PENDULUM PUTTER

The Pendulum putter, patented in the UK in 1907 by Reginald Marriott and Allen Ransome, has a triangular head that is used croquet style. The three sides of the head form three faces. Each one has a different loft for short putts, long putts, and chip shots.

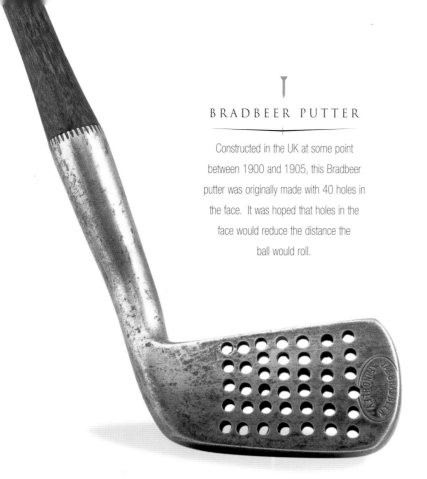

BRADBEER PUTTER

Constructed in the UK at some point between 1900 and 1905, this Bradbeer putter was originally made with 40 holes in the face. It was hoped that holes in the face would reduce the distance the ball would roll.

CROSSHEAD PUTTER

This unmarked crosshead putter has a steel face and a thick brass backweight. Two long screws in the back of the backweight extend completely through the head and are fastened to the metal face.

THOMPSON ADJUSTABLE

Rotating the long lever behind the hosel loosens the blade, which can adjust to three different lofts. The lever returns to its upright position when the blade is tight. Made from gunmetal, this club was patented in the US in 1901 by Eben Thompson of Massachusetts. It sold at a 1991 Sporting Antiquities auction for $6,000.

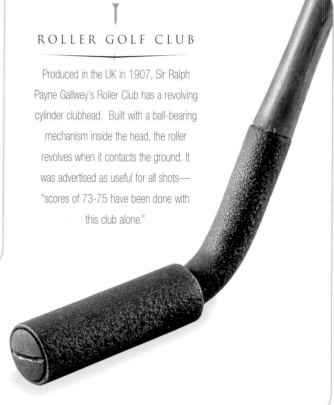

ROLLER GOLF CLUB

Produced in the UK in 1907, Sir Ralph Payne Gallwey's Roller Club has a revolving cylinder clubhead. Built with a ball-bearing mechanism inside the head, the roller revolves when it contacts the ground. It was advertised as useful for all shots— "scores of 73-75 have been done with this club alone."

TROPHY CLUB

This club was presented in 1903 to the Bromley & Bickley Golf Club, near London, by Herbert E. Bouch. The head is hallmarked sterling silver as is every band and ball on the shaft and the cap atop the grip. This club is one of two that served as perpetual trophies for an annual foursome competition. Each year, a ball and a band engraved with the winners' names were added to the shaft. The companion club to this iron sold privately in 1998 for $18,000.

SIMPLEX METALWOOD

This Simplex #5 is covered under Francis Brewster's 1907 British patent. Brewster wanted to cast his distinctive clubheads, originally patented in 1897 (see p. 74), in aluminum and still fasten the shaft in wood. He believed this would make construction easier and reduce costs.

1000 PUTTER

Robert Black "Buff" Wilson, of St. Andrews, developed his model 1000 putter by the end of 1901. The idea was to concentrate the weight in the center of the face. Along with the double "window" version shown, he produced a single window version with one square hole on the heel of the blade.

GIBSON PUTTER

Crafted by William Gibson of Kinghorn, Scotland, this putter is center-shafted in principle, but the hosel attaches to the heel of the blade. This design sets the face well in front of the shaft.

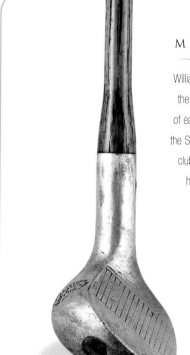

MILLS NK NIBLICK

William Mills of Sunderland, England, was the most prolific designer/manufacturer of early aluminum clubheads. He formed the Standard Golf Company to produce his clubs. The NK niblick was designed to handle sand bunkers and bad lies.

POPE'S PUTTER

Pope's putter was designed to enable the golfer to play the ball from the very center of the club face and in a direct line to the hole. Not only is the hosel flush with the face, it is centered between the heel and toe atop a rectangular head. W.R. Pope registered his club in the UK in 1904.

VARDON PUTTER

In 1904 John Carruthers received a British patent that covered this Vardon putter. Carruthers calculated that the curved face would redirect, and thereby correct, the errant shot accidentally struck on either the toe or heel.

KEMPSHALL PUTTER

The head of this Schenectady-style putter is made from laminated layers of white pyralin, a type of vulcanized rubber. Produced in 1904 by the Kempshall Manufacturing Company, of Arlington, New Jersey, this putter is much larger than most. Notice how large the head is in relation to the shaft.

SPALDING DRIVER

In his 1903 patent covering the center-shafted Schenectady putter, Arthur Knight includes a drawing of a proposed center-shafted driver nearly identical to the driver shown here. This club is stamped "A.G. Spalding & Bros." on the shaft. Spalding was one of the first companies to produce the Schenectady putter.

HIGGS DELIVERER

Registered in the UK by Robert Higgs in 1904, this rake iron was designed for use in sand, water, and long grass. Higg's calculated that these elements would pass through the face of the club when a stoke was made, thus increasing the force and accuracy of the stoke. Notice that the writing is located at the top of the blade. Genuine rake and water irons are marked *away* from their openings. In 1992 this club sold privately for $14,000.

TYKE PUTTER

This Tyke putter has a square wood head, a brass soleplate covering the entire sole, and four separate striking faces. The shaft is marked with the name of "D.M. Patrick," a clubmaker located at Lundin Links near Leven, Scotland.

SOLE-PLATE IRON

Francis Brewster received a British patent dated November 14, 1903, that covered his Sole-Plate irons. In the December 1904 issue of *Golfing*, Brewster's Simplex Golf Association advertised six different Sole-Plate irons. This example is the mashie niblick.

TYLECOATE'S PUTTER

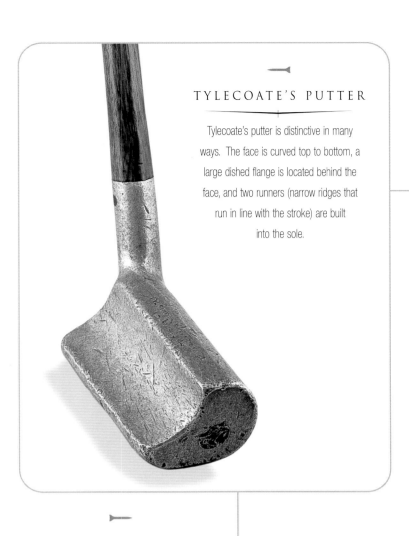

Tylecoate's putter is distinctive in many ways. The face is curved top to bottom, a large dished flange is located behind the face, and two runners (narrow ridges that run in line with the stroke) are built into the sole.

SWAN NECK PUTTER

Charles Seely's 1912 US patent covered the use of "steel tangs" in place of a hosel. James Brown's 1904 British patent covered a "swan neck," a bent hosel that lines up the shaft with the center of the head. This brass putter employs both features but was made prior to either patent. It sold at the 1991 Sporting Antiquities auction for $3,500.

ROGER BROWN IRON

Known as the "Roger Brown," this rake iron was covered under the 1904 British patent issued to James Roger of Glasgow, Scotland. Roger's club was produced in conjunction with J.R. Brown's rake irons; hence, it was named after James Roger and James Brown. In a 1992 Phillip's golf auction in Chester, England, a Roger Brown sold for $14,000.

SCHENECTADY PUTTERS

Made famous by Walter Travis when he won the British Amateur in 1904, the Schenectady putter was patented by Arthur Knight of Schenectady, New York, in 1903. The rear of the aluminum example on the right is marked "The Schenectady Putter / Patent Applied For." The rear of the cast iron model on the left is marked "Schenectady Putter #2."

MOORE BRASSEY

John Moore, a British clubmaker and greenkeeper, began making drivers and brassies with square shafts in 1902. Moore claimed that square shafts provided greater resistance from corner to corner, hence a square shaft would provide a straighter shot.

MCQUAKER PUTTER

This McQuaker center shaft putter has a cylindrical wood head inlaid with a circular ivory face insert and a circular lead back-weight. A golfer could use it right-handed, left-handed, or croquet style. In 2001 this club sold sold for $4500.

EVANS STYMIE PUTTER

In match play prior to 1952, a "stymie" occurred whenever player A's ball was directly in the path between player B's ball and the hole. Player B had to negotiate player A's ball and could not ask player A to remove his ball unless it was within 6 inches of player B's ball. Ronald Evans's croquet style putter, patented in the UK in 1908, includes a face designed to loft a ball on a stymied putt.

PALMER IRON & DRIVER

In 1901, Isaac Palmer received a US patent that covered his fork shaft clubs. Palmer calculated that his clubs would reduce the twisting of the head when striking the ball. After the craftsmen at Spalding made these clubs, they probably did not make any more, a "will not work" verdict being obvious.

BLACK PUTTER

This splice neck wooden putter with two rollers was patented in the UK in 1902 by Thomas Black. According to his patent, Black believed that the rollers would "prevent the stroke of the club from being spoiled by the head or sole of the club coming in contact with the ground or turf before reaching the ball, such a stroke being commonly known as 'duffing'." In 1993 a Black roller putter sold for $4,500.

BROWN RAKE IRONS

In 1903 James Brown received a British patent that covered his rake irons. Pictured left to right are Brown's Thistle, General, Major, and Perforated Cleek. Between 1990 and 2000, these models rarely came up for sale, but when they did they sold for $3,000 to $12,000 depending on condition, model, and market conditions.

ROBERTSON PUTTER

In 1903, Andrew Robertson received a British patent that covered a golf club with interchangeable heads. This Robertson putter screws together using left-handed threads, so striking the ball will only tighten the joint.

SPALDING PUTTER

This oversize croquet-style putter is a descendent from a "golf-croquet" club. Golf-croquet was a hybrid game devised by Henry McCrea around 1900. Spalding produced clubs for McCrea's game, but this putter, marked "Spalding," was made exclusively for golf.

THOMPSON & MITCHELL

This clubhead consists of an aluminum shell filled with gutta percha exposed at the face and in holes all over the head, including nine on the sole. According to the January 25,1906, US patent issued to Charles Thompson and Frank Mitchell for this club, the holes helped fasten the gutta percha in place.

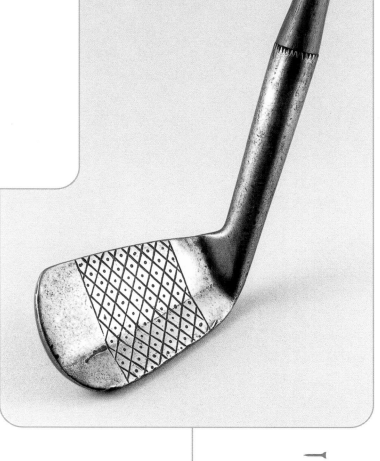

SHARPE'S MASHIE

Thomas Sharpe's 1906 British patent covered his dual face mashie and described it as able to provide increased backspin, negotiate stymies, and loft short pitch shots that would "fall very dead."

STRAIGHT DRIVING IRON

Arthur Tooley promoted his heel and toe weighted Straight Driving iron as able to "keep your ball perfectly straight" and "prevent pulling or slicing." In 1905, Tooley registered this club design in Great Britain.

Production methods did not change much for woods, irons, and putters during this period. World War I (1914-1918) had an adverse effect on the market, but there were still a few important innovations during this period. • In 1912 and 1913, Edwin Hamilton Winkworth Scott received two patents for a hollow steel shaft. His patents were not the first to deal with steel shafts, but his shafts were the first to go into production and receive significant exposure in the marketplace. Hamilton's shaft was square and, beginning in 1913, was sold installed in a putter of his own design. • In 1914 both the R&A and the USGA determined that steel shafts were illegal under existing rules. Steel shafts, however, were not to be denied. Between 1915 and 1920, Spalding used Scott's shaft in their Olympic putter. In 1918 and 1919, Spalding offered irons, and woods (by special order), with perforated steel shafts patented in 1915 and 1916 by Allen Lard. These shafts were bored out using a gun boring machine, then milled to provide six sides, then drilled with upwards of 1000 small holes to lighten the shaft. Even more steel shafts would follow in the ensuing years. • Just as the steel shaft began to gain approval and stir controversy, so, too, did the backspin iron. Backspin irons were made with unusually deep and wide grooves or other marks cut into the face. As their name implies, backspin irons were designed to increase the backspin imparted to the ball. Ben Sayers is often credited with inventing the and even crafted irons that were designed with the same purpose in mind, Sayers was the first to use oversized grooves. Other makers quickly followed and backspin irons were in widespread use by 1920. Golfers who used backspin irons did not use a whole set of them. They carried just one, or maybe two, for use on certain approach shots. Golf's governing bodies, however, were not at peace with such performance-enhancing clubs. The R&A outlawed backspin irons in 1921 followed by the USGA in 1924. • Golf balls made during this period were all of the rubber core variety. And they were getting better. Both the interior and exterior were constantly reinvented. Early rubber core balls used gutta percha covers, but manufacturers switched to rubber covers less prone to becoming brittle and cracking. Covers came in a wide variety of shapes and patterns. MacGregor's 1913 catalog offered balls with the following covers: recessed crescent shapes, diamonds, three-leaf clovers, triangles, raised bramble bumps, circular discs, rings with diamond shapes inside, and small pebble markings. Ball makers used a variety of cores such as liquid-filled, air-filled, solid rubber, glass, and even radioactive radium salts just to name a few.

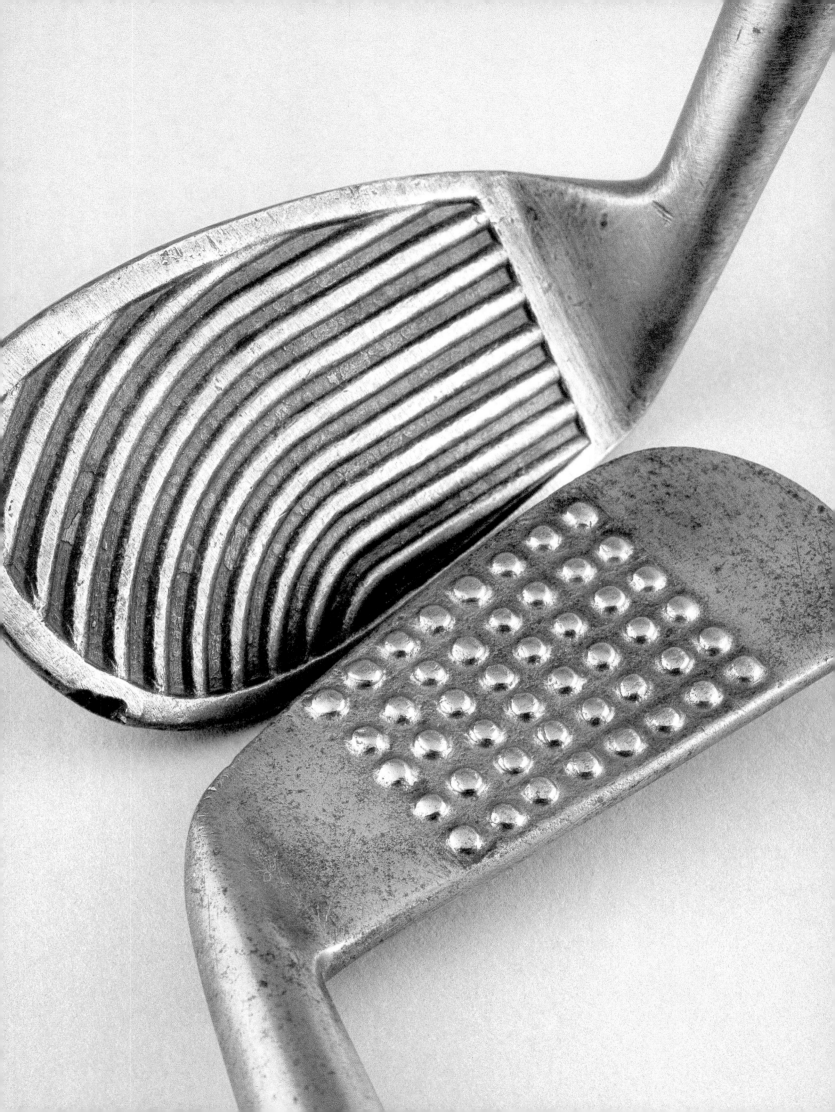

STRATE-PUT PUTTER

The Strate-Put has a duplex head, usable both left- and right-handed. A threaded screwcap can be removed at the toe to access a chamber inside the head where weight can be added or removed.

CANNON IRON

Walter Cannon received a British patent dated March 26, 1912, that covered this pointed-toe iron. A few other irons were made with similar toes, but only Cannon's pointed-toe iron had an *elliptical* head, the main feature covered in his patent.

SAMSON IRON

According to Philip Samson's 1911 British patent, the insert in this iron is made from woven fabric, such as cotton, wool, jute, hemp, asbestos, etc. The fabric was impregnated with "a binding substance" to make it waterproof and elastic.

DEMON DRIVER

Horace Hutchison, winner of the 1886 and
1887 British Amateur titles, received a
patent in 1892 that covered a club nearly
identical to the one shown here. This driver
is marked "The Demon" along with a six
digit British design registration number
that dates to 1912.

STRAIGHTSHOT PUTTER

The face on this iron putter, made by
Robert Brodie & Sons, consists of a circular
disc, only 1 3/8 inches in diameter, placed
half an inch ahead of an otherwise ordinary
blade. A vertical brace formed integrally
with the back of the disc is attached to
the center of the blade. All the brass
examples of this putter are fakes.

WATER IRON

Because this David Stephenson water iron
was originally made with thirteen holes
through the face, all the marks on the back
of the head are located well away from the
center of the blade. Stamping the head
was the last step in making an iron.

RAKE IRONS

The light-colored head is marked "Atlas Co. / The Rake." Produced in the UK, this head appears to use nickel as its primary metal. It is much heavier than aluminum and is non-magnetic. This club sold privately in 1994 for $5,000. The dark head is marked "Ben Knight" low across the back. Between 1911 and 1920, Knight worked as a pro in Michigan and Iowa.

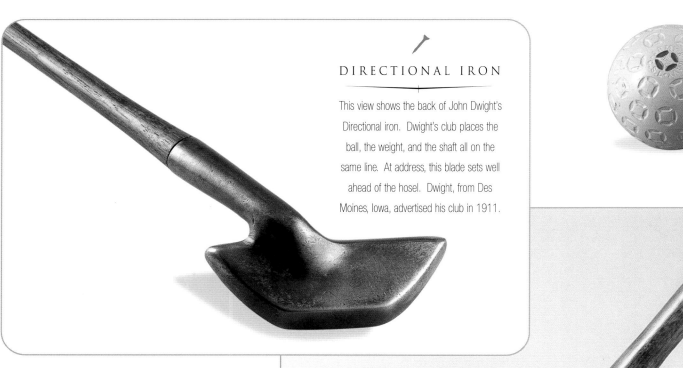

DIRECTIONAL IRON

This view shows the back of John Dwight's Directional iron. Dwight's club places the ball, the weight, and the shaft all on the same line. At address, this blade sets well ahead of the hosel. Dwight, from Des Moines, Iowa, advertised his club in 1911.

LEGH DRIVING CLUB

Gilbert Legh's 1906 and 1910 British patents covered this club. Legh calculated that hollowing out the wood behind the metal face plate would provide a spring-face effect, and a short hosel would take full advantage of the shaft's flexibility.

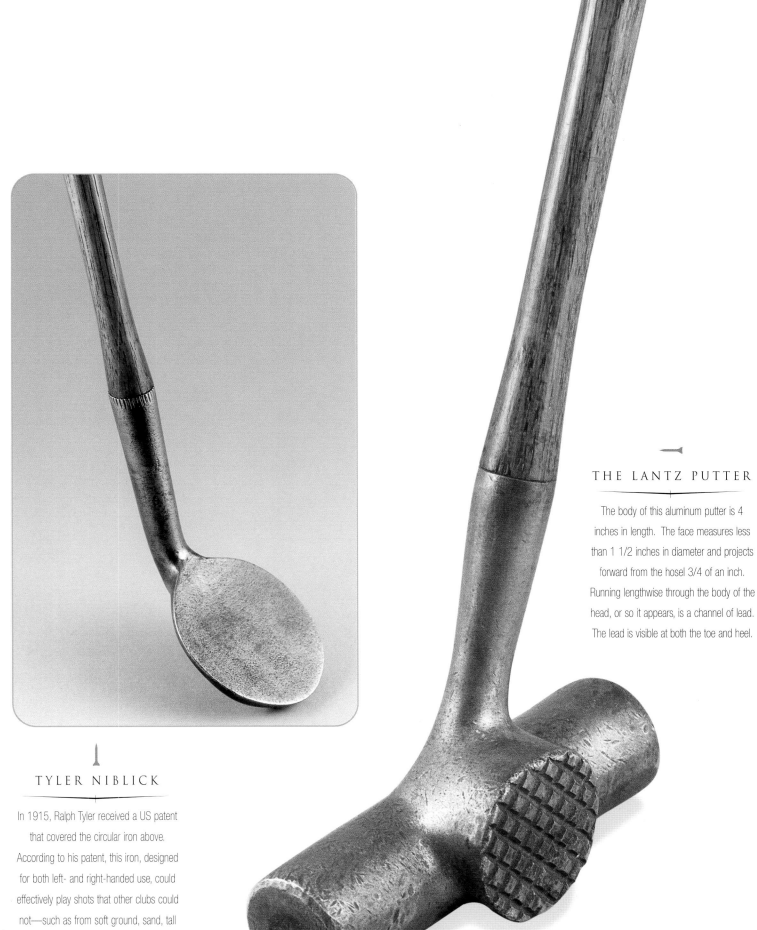

THE LANTZ PUTTER

The body of this aluminum putter is 4
inches in length. The face measures less
than 1 1/2 inches in diameter and projects
forward from the hosel 3/4 of an inch.
Running lengthwise through the body of the
head, or so it appears, is a channel of lead.
The lead is visible at both the toe and heel.

TYLER NIBLICK

In 1915, Ralph Tyler received a US patent
that covered the circular iron above.
According to his patent, this iron, designed
for both left- and right-handed use, could
effectively play shots that other clubs could
not—such as from soft ground, sand, tall
grass, a small hollow, a long narrow hollow,
beneath an overhanging rock, beneath the
lower board of a fence, behind the lip of a
bunker, or in any other difficult place.

ANDERSON PUTTER

The cork face, devised to cushion the blow at impact, extends through the head and is visible across the back. Offered by Spalding between 1915 and 1920, the "Cork Center" putter was patented in the US in 1914 by Lewis Anderson.

HACKBARTH PUTTER

Otto Hackbarth of St. Louis, Missouri, claimed that the fork hosel prevented his putter from turning when the ball was struck. Hackbarth putters were first advertised in 1910 and made famous by Chick Evans, lifelong amateur and 1916 US Open champ.

EMERGENCY IRON

This mechanical club has three different striking faces. To adjust the head, loosen the screw at the toe, pull the head away from the hosel, rotate the head to the desired side, push the head back in, then tighten the screw. In 1915 and 1917, Louis Vories received two US patents for this iron. In 1993 a Vories iron sold for $3200 at auction.

MASTER GOLF CLUB

This adjustable iron, patented by William Breitenbaugh in the US in 1915, works by using a nut on a threaded blade stem that extends through the hosel. Both sides of the blade are scored, so the head can be used either right-side-up or upside-down.

DEDSTOP MASHIE

Offered in Spalding's Oct. 5, 1919 catalog, this "double waterfall" iron was patented in the US in 1920 by William Reach. Despite many known examples, double waterfall irons have sold for upwards of $4,000.

ANDERSON PUTTER

This putter measures 6 inches across the face, not including the hosel. It was made by Alex Anderson of Anstruther, Scotland, and was sold sometime between 1910 and 1915 by D.P Watt, a professional in Edinburgh, Scotland.

HARDRIGHT DRIVER

Hardright Drivers are made from condensite, the invention of J.W. Aylesworth who was Thomas Edison's chief chemist for 25 years. Condensite is made from a black, hardened gum. Hardright drivers were made with either a standard pinned shaft or a screw-in shaft as shown here.

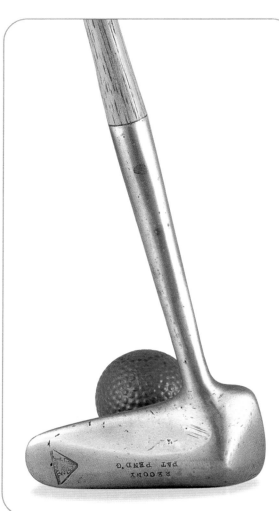

DED-STOP IRON

The shaft in this Spalding Ded-Stop iron was covered under Allan Lard's 1915 and 1916 US patents. The shaft is made from a solid piece of steel that was bored out and milled to create six sides. It was then drilled with upwards of 1,000 holes. Between 1990-2000, ordinary Lard shaft irons sold for $3,000-$5000.

RECONY PUTTER

This circa 1915 backwards putter, has a head that extends underneath the hosel back *towards* the golfer. It was made from monel metal (67% nickel, 28% copper, 5% other metals) by the Monel Metal Products Corp. of Bayonne, New Jersey.

MOLINE METALWOOD

"Patent App For / Moline, Ill" is the only writing on this otherwise anonymous metalwood. Two screws in the back of the head and one in the sole hold the fiber insert in place. It appears unlikely that a patent was issued.

FITZJOHN PUTTER

The hosel on this putter is easily adjusted to suit the desires of any golfer. The golfer need only loosen the screw on the back of the head, adjust the shaft to its new position, and then tighten the screw. Usable left-handed, right-handed, or croquet style, this gunmetal putter was covered under a 1917 US patent granted to Edward Fitzjohn and Elmer Stanton. This club sold privately in 2001 for $6,500.

KELLY DRIVER

According to the 1913 US patent issued to John Kelly and Patrick McCardle for this ball-shaped metalwood, this club was designed to be a universal club. It accepts various inserts, each having a different loft, and the golfer need only unscrew the shaft to change the insert.

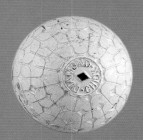

COLLINS DRIVER

This driver, covered under Stephen Collins and Harold Pearce's 1911 British patent, contains a measuring mechanism: the harder the ball hits the spring-loaded face, the further back the disk atop the head moves. The more off-center the hit, the more the disk rotates.

ADJUSTABLE IRON

Pulling up on the lever on the back of the head loosens the blade, which can then be rotated to the desired loft. Pressing the lever back down locks the blade in place. This circa 1910 club is unmarked.

NON-SKID CLEEK

The raised "bramble" bumps on the face were supposed to prevent the ball from skidding off the face. This iron, covered under Joshua Taylor's 1912 British patent, sold for $5,000 at a July 2000 Christie's auction in London.

MITEE PUTTER

The sole of this duplex putter is "V" shaped. Each face is formed by the edge where the sole meets the bevelled crown, which is marked "William Burke's The Original Hand Made / Mitee Putter / Pat Applied For." The ball is struck by the ridge formed where the sole meets the beveled edge.

XL METALWOOD

Turning a screw in the back of the XL head adjusts the tension of a spring located inside the head, increasing or decreasing the resilience of the spring-loaded face. In 1912, George Wilford received a British patent for this club. Wilford calculated that a resilient face would recoil and thereby add distance to a drive. This club sold for $6,000 at a July 1991 Sotheby's golf auction.

ONE-O-ONE PUTTER

The top of this putter is marked "One-O-One" along with "Jakwyte." The term Jakwyte is obviously a play on the name of Jack White, the 1904 British Open champion, but the connection between White and this putter is not known. A Jakwyte One-O-One putter sold at a July 2000 Christie's auction for $5,000.

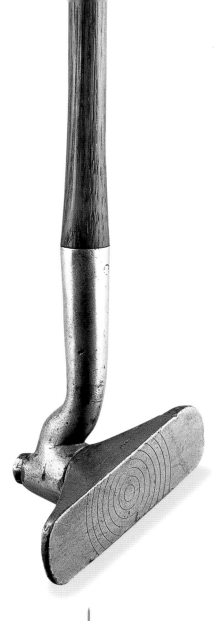

GASSIAT PUTTER

Originally called the Chantilly putter, after Chantilly, France, the home of its inventor the Marquis de Chasseloup-Loubat, this putter became known as the Gassiat putter. Jean Gassiat was the professional in Chantilly who won the French Open four times. In 1913, W. M. Winton received a British design registration for this club.

FITZJOHN PUTTER

The mechanical head on this Fitzjohn putter operates the same way as the head on the Fitzjohn putter shown on page 105 although they have different shapes. This club sold at the 1992 Sporting Antiquities auction for $4,700.

THE FACILE PUTTER

David Wilson, the professional and club-maker for the London Scottish Golf Club, received a British design registration for this putter on January 23, 1912. It was thought that a flange atop the putter would help impart top-spin to the ball.

DIRECTIONAL DRIVER

A US patent dated May 12, 1914, was issued to John Dwight for his "cow's horn" driver, advertised as Dwight's Directional driver. Dwight designed the sole of his driver so the golfer could increase the trajectory of a shot by leaning the the shaft back. A Directional driver sold privately in 1999 for $7,500.

OLYMPIC PUTTER

This square metal shaft was covered under two British patents issued to Edward Scott in 1912 and 1913. Spalding offered this putter between 1915 and 1920.

REES WIZARD PUTTER

Patented in the US in 1916 by George Rees, this putter has a telescoping alignment rod that fits inside the head when not in use. To deploy the rod as shown, simply push down the plate on the back of the bronze head and watch the spring-loaded rod automatically swing out into position. The rod extends to three times its collapsed length. In 1989 a Rees Wizard sold for $7,500.

TAYLOR RAKE

According to Thomas Taylor's 1910 US patent, his rake iron has a series of "feet like miniature flat irons." Taylor believed this sole would offer less wind resistance and reduce pulling, slicing, and topping. This iron sold for $10,000 in 1992.

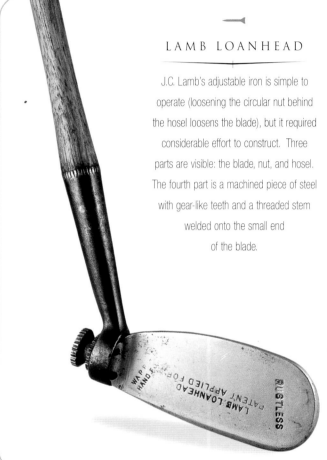

LAMB LOANHEAD

J.C. Lamb's adjustable iron is simple to operate (loosening the circular nut behind the hosel loosens the blade), but it required considerable effort to construct. Three parts are visible: the blade, nut, and hosel. The fourth part is a machined piece of steel with gear-like teeth and a threaded stem welded onto the small end of the blade.

WOODFACE PUTTER

William Gibson's circa 1910 Woodface putter is of the Smith-neck anti-shank variety. The wood face is held in place by four screws, one in each corner. Each screw tip is visible on the face.

WOODFACE PUTTER

Made with a wood face on an aluminum head, this putter sought to circumvent the the 1910 R&A ban on Schenectady putters. Instead of being located in the center of the head, the hosel on this unmarked putter is at the very back of the head which keeps the shaft on axis with the sweetspot.

METALWOOD DRIVER

A large, circular, wood dowel forms the center of the face of this driver. It extends through the head and is visible on the back, as shown. A second, smaller wood dowel extends into the head from the toe in order to help fasten the larger dowel in place. This club is unmarked. Its creator is unknown.

SIMPSON BRASSEY

Split cane shafts, made from a number of lengthwise pieces of bamboo, were tried on a long nose club or two as well as on a number of clubs made during the 1920s and 1930s. The shaft in this circa 1910 Robert Simpson brassey, however, was originally made from a solid piece of cane.

ALL-ONE CLUBS

Turning the hosel nut on the iron far left raises a rod (inside the hosel) out of the blade so the blade can be moved to a new loft. Lifting the hosel lever on the other iron does the same thing. Both clubs were covered under Charles Curry's 1914 US patent. The iron far left was also covered under Latimer Goodrich's 1918 US Patent.

DEADUN IRON

In 1914 Jack White, the 1904 British Open champion, introduced his Civic putter, which had 24 holes drilled in the face. Shortly thereafter he devised his Deadun iron. Both clubs were supposed to deaden the ball at impact and thereby reduce the distance the ball would roll.

TEDDER PUTTER

On July 27, 1912, Walter Tedder, a British professional in Nottingham, received a British design registration that covered this putter. Years later, a putter modeled after this one—the Jonko (p. 133)—was produced by William Gibson.

JUMBO DRIVER

The face on this unmarked circa 1910 driver measures a full 2 5/8 inches from top to bottom. According to a 1908 advertisement, Ben Sayers was the only maker of Jumbo drivers at this time.

2-PIECE PUTTER

On this unmarked circa 1910 putter, the mallet head and the neck are separate pieces. Removing the screw in the sole allowed the golfer to disassemble the club. This joint made it easy for the golfer to switch to heads of different styles, all made by the same maker, of course.

T-FRAME PUTTER

Made from either brass or gunmetal, this unmarked circa 1910 putter is cast, not forged. It is hollow and pings when tapped on either the blade or alignment bar. This club sold privately in 1993 for $3500.

Between 1920 and 1924, several golf manufacturers and retailers offered steel shaft golf clubs even though steel shafts were considered illegal by the USGA and R&A. Clubmakers had long been worried about the diminishing supply of quality hickory from which to produce shafts. Metal shafts were perceived as unlimited in supply, less costly to inventory, easier to work with, more durable, and game enhancing. • Effective April 12, 1924, the USGA passed a resolution permitting the use of steel shafts. The Bristol Manufacturing Company, the Union Hardware Company, American Fork & Hoe Company (which became the True Temper Corporation), and the Kroydon Company took the lead in steel shaft production. • Steel shafts grew in popularity, but clubmakers did not stop producing hickory shaft clubs. Instead, they offered both hickory shaft clubs and steel shaft clubs. A sizable number of golfers, however, felt that hickory was not only traditional, it was proven. Even the great Bobby Jones used only hickory shafts throughout the 1920s and was still using them in 1930 when he won the Grand Slam. • To boost the appeal of steel shafts to the traditional golfer, clubmakers began to sheathe the shafts in a flexible celluloid/thermoplastic tubing called pyratone. It was often colored to imitate wood grain. Many of these shafts looked so much like wood that, even today, the unknowing often mistake pyratone-covered shafts for wood shafts. • Prior to 1926, the golfer usually assembled a set of irons by choosing individual clubs, often from various makers, even though sets of four or five clubs were available. In 1926, Spalding, to name one manufacturer, first offered a full set of irons for a single price. During the mid to late 1920s, clubmakers continued to sell individual irons while they increased their promotion of matched sets, often including the putter. Within a few years, most golfers were purchasing sets of both woods and irons. • The concept of swing-weighting clubs was introduced during this period. On November 24, 1924, Irving R. Prentis of Philadelphia, Pennsylvania, received a US patent for his method of balancing clubs—of properly proportioning them from one to the next—within a set. Robert Adams, of Waban, Massachusetts, created a "lorythmic" scale based on Prentis's method, and Kenneth Smith marketed the scale, which remains in use to this day. • In 1920 the R&A, in tandem with the USGA, established the size of a golf ball at 1.62 inches in diameter and 1.62 ounces in weight. Prior to this, rules governing the size and weight of a golf ball did not exist. Balls continued to be made with rubber cores wound tighter and tighter. In the late 1920s both US Rubber and Spalding devised a process to vulcanize (harden) the balata cover used on balls, which improved their playability as well as stability. The ball not only went farther, but it was now less likely to crack or break open. Most of the balls produced during this era had square mesh dimples or round dimples, although ball makers continued to produce the occasional unusual cover pattern or core material.

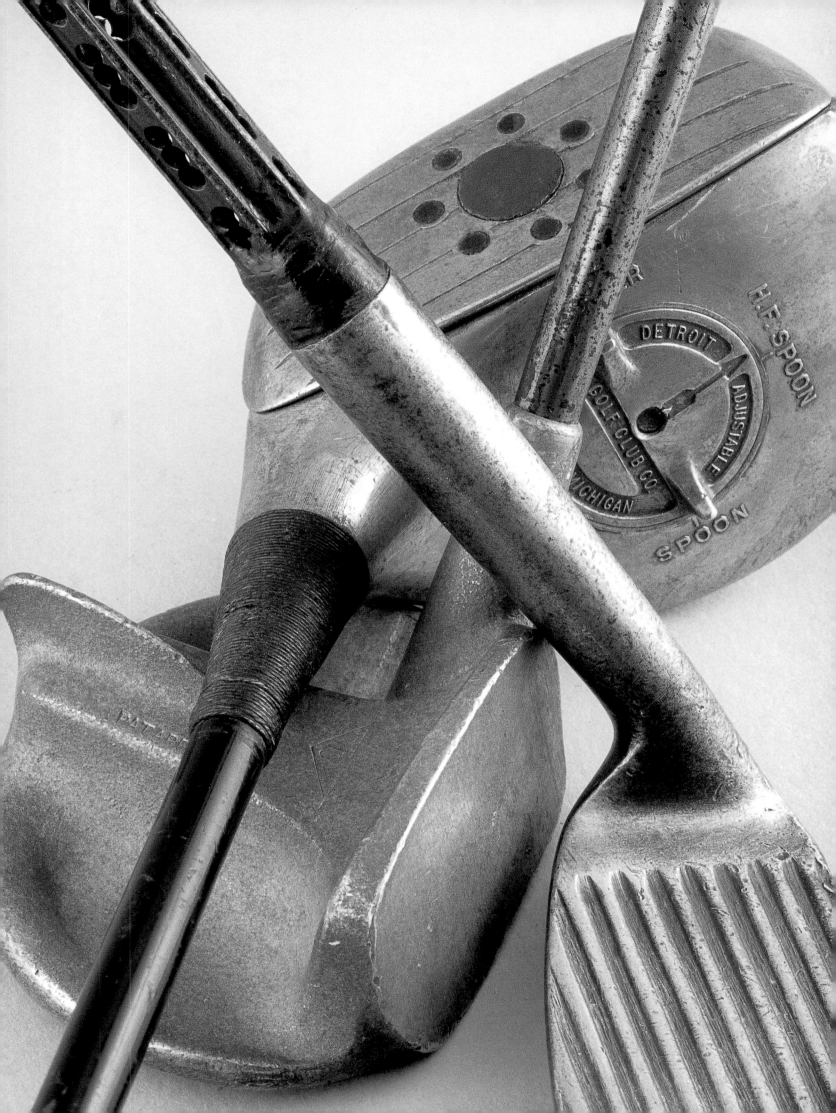

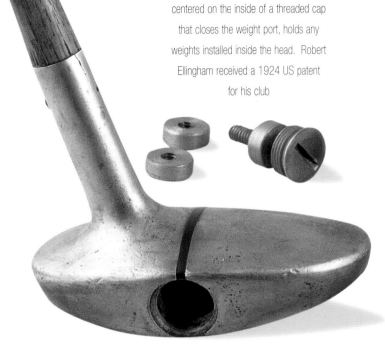

ELLINGHAM PUTTER

Ellingham's putter includes a weight port located midway across the back of its Schenectady-style head. A threaded rod, centered on the inside of a threaded cap that closes the weight port, holds any weights installed inside the head. Robert Ellingham received a 1924 US patent for his club

MAC & MAC PUTTER

This pointed back putter was advertised in 1923 by Mac & Mac, a small company in Oak Park, Illinois. The head is made from German silver, also known as nickel silver. The shaft was made square to help the golfer's alignment.

LINDGREN DUPLEX

Walfred Lindgren's 1926 US patent covered his adjustable duplex club. The cross-scored straight face shown was used for putting; the line-scored lofted face on the opposite side of the head allowed the club to function as a midiron. The hosel tilts back and forth so either face can be used right-handed, left-handed, or croquet-style.

McCLAIN SAND WEDGE

On December 18, 1928, Edwin McClain received a US patent for his Sand Wedge. McClain's club met with quick acceptance. Bobby Jones even used one in winning the 1930 British Open. In 1931, the USGA declared the concave face illegal. Others quickly designed flat face sand wedges that used large cambered soles similar to the one McClain devised.

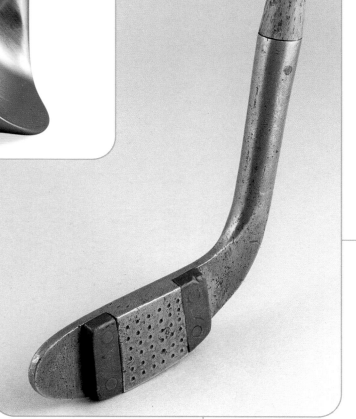

YOUNG PUTTER

Designed to help the golfer's alignment, the striking face on this putter projects forward ahead of the blade. To accommodate mis-hit putts, strips of red fiber, fastened in place by two brass rivets, border the face. The back of the blade is marked "Jack Young / Hand Made Special." Young worked as a professional in New York, Pennsylvania, and Connecticut between 1922 and 1928.

GUERNE METALWOOD

The white insert across the face is a porcelain block set in vulcanized rubber. The block extends halfway back into the head. Inside the rear of the head is a rod with threaded weights. The shaft consists of six lengthwise pieces of bamboo around a hickory core. In 1925 Alfred Guerne received a US patent for the insert and weight system in his club.

ALLEN DUPLEX

Allen's hosel pivots back and forth, heel to toe, in order to make the club usable right-handed, left-handed, or croquet style. Rotating the gunmetal hosel loosens the head or locks it into position. The front of Allen's clubhead provides a flat putting face. The back of the head, which is shown, provides a dual-lofted face for chipping. Edwin Allen's 1924 US patent covered the adjustable mechanism on his club.

SUTTON PUTTER

This aluminum head putter, with three rollers on the sole, was produced in the late 1920s by Harry L. Sutton. The rollers were used to keep the head up to speed on stubbed putts. Remove the screws in the sole, and the rollers can be replaced with a solid piece.

MECHANICAL CLUB

Releasing the spring-loaded lever behind the hosel loosens the triangle head which can then be rotated to the desired face. This mid 1920s steel-shafted head has three faces usable right- or left-handed.

EVANS PUTTER

Chick Evans, a lifelong amateur and one of the greatest ever, won both the US Open and US Amateur in 1916. He enjoyed a special relationship with Thomas E. Wilson & Company wherein he remained an amateur. This club, marked with both the name of Evans and Wilson, was not made for resale.

STERLING PUTTER

The head on this Walter Hagen putter, a replica of the one Hagen used to win four open championships, was made from sterling silver by Lambert Brothers Jewellers, New York. Hagen sterling putters, first advertised in 1925 and suitable for use, were primarily given as a gift or tournament prize.

TURNER PUTTER

The metal hosel on this putter is integral with the metal frame running through the head. Two shaped wood blocks attached to the frame form the front and rear of the head. Produced in the UK in the early 1920s by Sherlock, Ray & Turner, this club has a ram's horn slip, not a soleplate.

WORTHINGTON IRON

To overcome the tendency to "dig in," George Worthington designed this mid-iron with a large cambered sole that extends well behind the blade. When contacting the ground, the sole would tend to lift the club-head out of the sod. In 1927 Worthington received a US patent for his flange sole irons which he made out of aluminum in order to keep the weight manageable.

PEDERSON IRON

According to Walter Pederson's 1925 US patent, the convex face of his iron would allow the ball a "continued engagement" with the face at impact and would therefore, as the ball rolled up the face, impart additional backspin.

OLSON PUTTER

The shaft on Olson's putter can rotate to any usable position left-handed, right-handed, croquet style, or shuffleboard style. Simply tilt the shaft to the desired position —no loosening or tightening of anything. In 1920 Andrew Olson received a US patent for this putter.

CALAMITY JANE

During his career, Bobby Jones used two Calamity Jane putters. Due to wear on the face, Jones retired his original model in 1926 and had six copies made for him by J. Victor East at Spalding. Marked "Rob't T. Jones Jr.," the putter shown is the actual Calamity Jane II that Jones used to win 10 of his 13 major championships. In 1938 Jones donated it to the USGA where it remains on display.

PEDERSON METALWOOD

Sporting a streamlined, clean look, Walter Pederson's metalwood was covered under a US patent issued on February 8, 1927. According to his patent, the three wood dowels visible across the top of the head help fasten a block of wood inside the head. The sole is rounded, and the brass soleplate is keyed into position.

PAMBO THE 2ND

Unbelieveable as it seems, J.B. Fulford devised this cylinder clubhead, which he named "Pambo the 2nd," to play all shots from tee to green. In 1920 he advertised that his club would not cut the ball and that it would not limit the distance obtained by the golfer—drives of 250 yards often being obtained. The original Pambo was a similar cylinder head putter.

4-WAY DRIVER

Turning the circular nut atop the red plastic head loosens the head, which can then be rotated to position any of its four sides as the striking face. Each side of this steel shaft clubhead has a different loft.

RUDDER PUTTER

According to a 1923 ad, the Rudder putter was made to help "the person who accepts a steady diet of three's on the green." It would provide not only direction, but also a sense of distance. The Rudder putter was sold by Holmac Inc. of New York.

SLOG-EM 2 IRON

In 1928, Thomas Todrick received a British patent for this removable clubhead, which is threaded at the top to fit a threaded collar. When the head is put on the shaft, the hosel's thin walls and four lengthwise cuts allow the hosel to crimp down on the shaft as the collar is screwed down.

STEWART PUTTER

This late 1920s backwards putter was made by Tom Stewart of St. Andrews. It was sold by Willie Kidd, the professional at Interlachen Country Club in Edina, Minnesota.

SUITALL PUTTER

The rounded sole of the Suitall putter allows the clubhead to lie comfortably at any angle. The raised point on the center of the top of the blade aids alignment. Arthur Tooley received a British design registration for this club in 1924. This club sold privately in 2000 for $2500.

RITCHIE JUMBO DRIVER

In addition to having a face that measures an incredible 2 3/8 inches in depth, this clubhead is triangular in shape. William Ritchie produced this club shortly after becoming the professional at Addington, England, in 1922.

SPITTAL SHAFT

In 1928 David Spittal from Quebec, Canada, received a US patent that covered this half wood, half steel shaft. The upper half of the shaft is made from solid wood; the lower half is made from copper-coated tubular steel with a wood core. The wood from the upper half of the shaft extends down through the steel portion.

LEVEN IRON

This Leven iron is designed to measure how far a golfer's practice swing would have hit a ball. The spring-loaded measuring mechanism inside the hosel moves when the club is swung. The indicator, visible through a slot in the hosel, shows the author's practice swing was good for 70 yards (the ball didn't go as far in 1922). Push the button to reset the mechanism.

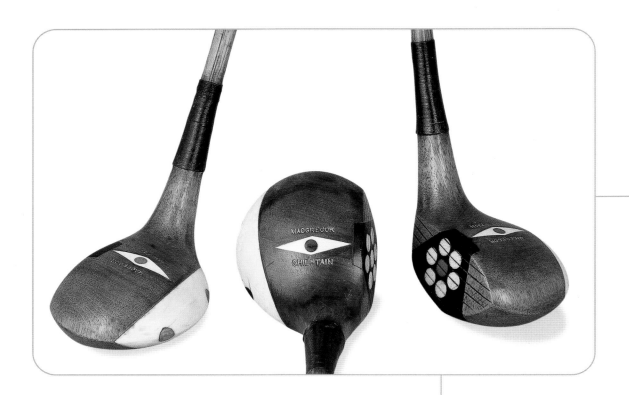

CHIEFTAIN WOOD SET

Made by MacGregor between 1927 and 1929, Chieftain woods have ivory inserts in the face, ivory inlays on the crown, ivory backweights, and brass soleplates. The black, green, and red dots identify the driver, brassie and spoon, respectively. These colored dots are threaded Scruloc inserts made from galalith, a casein product made from goat's milk.

SWAN PUTTER

In 1928, Donald Swan received a US patent that covered this putter, complete with a deep face and a triangular flange that projects *forward* from the *top* of the blade. The flange on Swan's putter was designed to obscure most of the ball, coming to a point above the ball as pictured.

RITZ DUPLEX

The Ritz, patented in the US in 1924 by George Reitenour, is designed for both left- and right-handed use. Both faces are identical and are filled with lead, the lead connecting through holes bored in the center of the head between the faces.

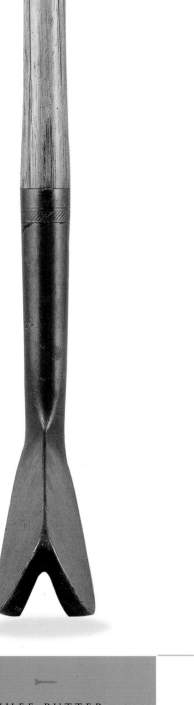

DUPLEX IRON

John Radel received a US patent dated October 2, 1928, that covered this duplex iron. The blades connect at the top-line and nowhere else: the entire underside of the club is open.

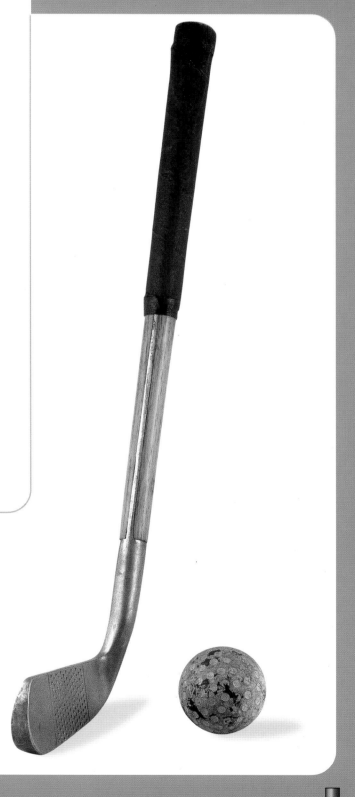

WHEE PUTTER

The Whee putter, produced in 1924 by R. Forgan & Son, measures only 14 inches in overall length. It was used for putting one-handed. A flat metal core, integral with the head, runs up the length of the shaft and is visible down the front and back of the shaft. Two rivets are used to affix the hickory to the sides of the flat metal core.

ONE-ARM DRIVER

This club, marked "Earnest Sales / Sunningdale," was made for a golfer having only one arm, most likely a golfer maimed in World War I. The exceptionally long 5 1/2 inch head and short 35 1/2 inch total length made contacting the ball easier for such a golfer.

LEVEN DRIVER

The Leven driver measures how far a golfer's practice swing would have hit a golf ball. This Leven driver and the Leven iron on page 123 work the same way and were patented in the UK in 1922 by Charles Leven. Swinging the club causes a small triangular marker inside the mechanism to register the yardage as marked on the cover plate. Push the button to reset.

GATKE SPRINGY SHAFT

A coiled spring low on the painted wood shaft is held in place by two long metal collars, one above and one below the spring. In 1925 Thomas Gatke received a US patent for this club, devised to improve the golfer's tempo.

PEARSON IRONS

Pearson mashies and niblicks fit into the rake/water iron category but they were designed for an additional purpose: back-spin. Produced by Mac & Mac, Pearson irons were made from granger steel but, according to their 1923 ads, were not guaranteed against breakage on shots longer than 75 yards!

HINGED SHAFT

The hinge in this Nicoll Bigshooter iron is strategically placed. Swing the club correctly and the shaft will stay rigid (the hinge will not move), allowing the golfer to strike the ball. This practice club is similar to the modern day Medicus swing trainer.

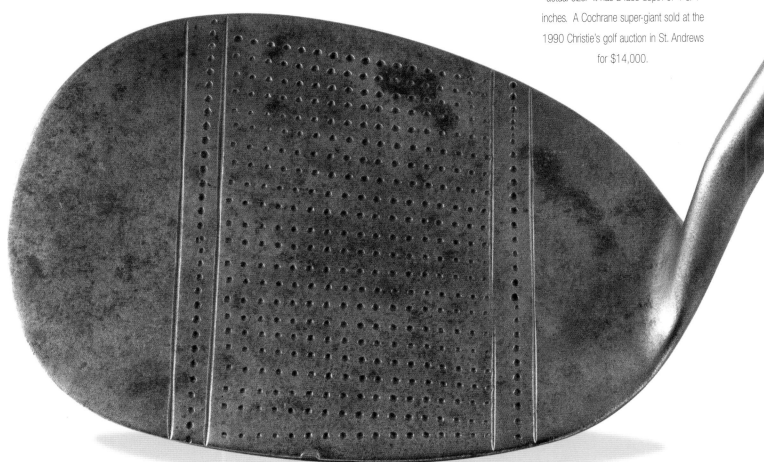

COCHRANE NIBLICK

During the 1920s a number of different clubmakers produced giant niblicks with oversize clubheads that measured between 3 1/8 and 3 7/8 inches in face depth. The ultimate in giant niblicks, however, is Cochrane's super-giant niblick, shown actual size. It has a face depth of 4 3/4 inches. A Cochrane super-giant sold at the 1990 Christie's golf auction in St. Andrews for $14,000.

F.H. AYRES 4 IRON

On December 8, 1926, F.H. Ayres, Ltd, London, received a British design registration for this club. The split back design of the head was adopted by MacGregor and used on the vast majority of the popular Tommy Armour irons made in America between 1935 and 1965.

TRIANGULAR PUTTER

The Triangular Adjustable Putter, produced
in 1923 by the Baltimore Putter Company,
is actually six putters in one. Each side of
the triangular head is a striking face with a
different loft, and the head rotates so that
three faces can be used by right-handed
players and three by left-handed players.

DUPLEX METALWOOD

This early steel shaft metalwood is
designed for both left- and right-handed
use. The left-handed face bears a
December 1925 patent date, but the day
is unreadable. This club sold at the 1992
Sporting Antiquities auction for $1500.

BOYE PUTTER/CHIPPER

The hosel on James Boye's putter tilts
back and forth, allowing for left-handed,
right-handed, or croquet style use. Boye's
1922 US patent, however, covers the back
of the head (shown) which is designed to
be a dual face chipper. The lower portion
of the face lofts the ball, and the upper-most
portion, curling forward with negative loft, is
also supposed to contact the ball and
remove all backspin so the
chip shot will run true.

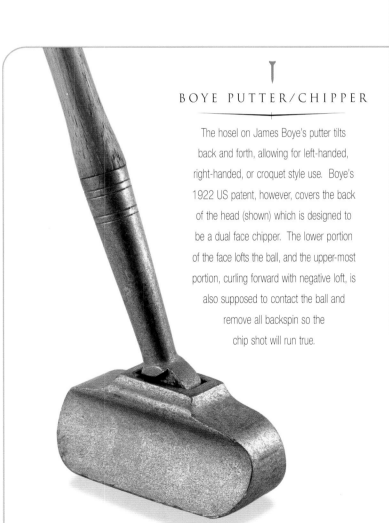

WONDER CLUBS

Waverly Horton designed three different
versions of his Wonder Club. Trying to
combine the durability of metal with the feel
of wood, Horton received a US patent
for his clubs in 1920.

TOUSEY RING SHAFT

According to both of Sinclair Tousey's
1922 US patents covering this club, the
raised rings spaced one inch apart along
the entire shaft would eliminate the
"objectionable" noise resulting from the
rapid motion of a golf club through the air
and increase the speed of the swing,
thereby providing longer drives.

ARDEN AERO CLUB

In the late 1920s, the Arden Company
promoted the futuristic Aero club as able to
"slaughter the slice." The copper-coated
steel shaft is the Bristol "Gold Label" shaft
made by the Horton Mfg. Co.

LAMINO DRIVER

Not only is the head of this driver made
from laminated wood, the shaft is, too. It is
difficult to see the lengthwise strips of wood
in the shaft because the grain does not
alternate from one strip to the next, as it
does in the head. Lamino shafts and
heads were covered under Harry Jordan's
1923 and 1925 US patents.

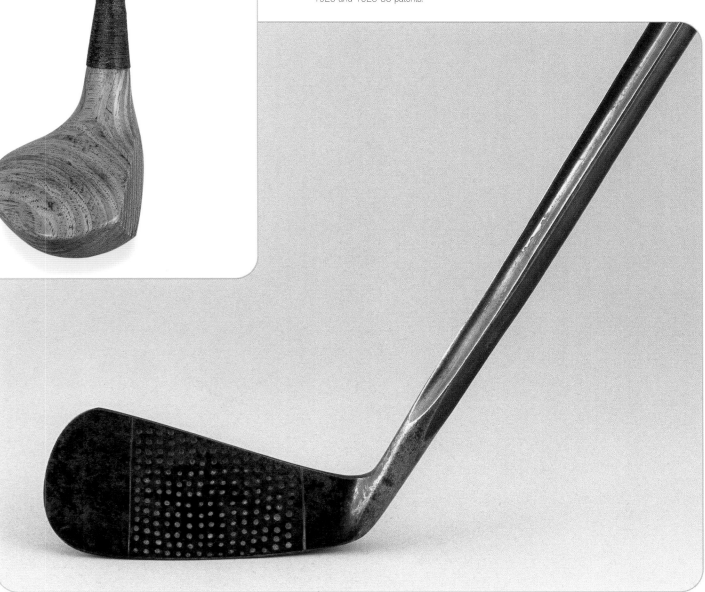

WHISTLER IRON

This entire iron is made from a single piece
of steel. It is the first golf shaft ever produced by American Fork and Hoe, which
later became True Temper. The Whistler,
nicknamed by company employees, was
covered under a patent issued to Robert
Cowdery in 1926 but applied for in 1922.

MARTIN PUTTER

This putter is, without a doubt, one of the worst ever designed. The blade, which is usable either right- or left-handed, comes to a point centered on the ridge running down the middle of the hosel. Therefore, the blade lines up right of the target for right-handed golfers and left of the target for left-handed golfers. Cyril J. M. Martin received a British design registration dated November 17, 1920, for this creation.

SAND WEDGE

Marked "Pat. Pend.," this *wooden* sand wedge has a dramatically curved face and bears the names of Walter Hagen and Beckley-Ralston. This club was probably related to the Hagen concave Sand Wedge (p. 117) and produced in 1930. When concave faces became illegal in 1931, there was little reason to complete the patent application on this club.

SCOTT PUTTER

The narrow, flat ridge running across the front of this putter projects well forward and serves as the striking face. When this A.H. Scott ridge face putter is placed behind the ball, the ridge corresponds to the center of the ball.

McDOUGAL PUTTER

This circa 1926 Albert McDougal putter has two chambers and indvidual lead weights, allowing the golfer to adjust its weight and balance.

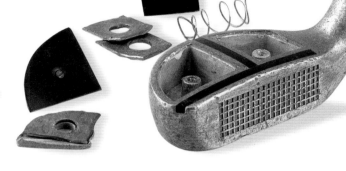

SCOTT PUTTER

Crafted by Andrew H. Scott, this cylinder putter is made from wood. It has a distinct guide mark on the crown. A copper plate covers the sole.

JONKO PUTTER

This Jonko putter was made by William Gibson of Kinghorn, Scotland. The original Jonko-style putter was designed by Ted Tedder and registered in 1912 (see p. 112). Gibson made a few Jonko putters with steel shafts in the late 1920s.

Cosmetics took on a larger role in golf club design during the late 1920s as clubmakers turned their attention to making golf clubs more attractive. No longer was it enough to produce a well-made club. It had to have a distinctive look. This element continued to develop through the 1930s, especially in the production of "fancy face" woods with colorful inserts. • On fancy face woods, the insert had a colorful design and sometimes consisted of a number of bright contrasting colors. In every instance the pattern was designed with the hope that golfers would find it attractive and inspiring—attractive enough to buy the club and inspiring enough to use it well. • Woods took a structural step forward during the 1940s. Drivers were made with deeper faces and fairway woods became more compact. MacGregor Golf led the way, producing a number of models with persimmon heads and attractive shapes that were prized until the rise of the metal wood in the 1980s. MacGregor's 693 woods, introduced in 1949, are considered by many top golfers to have the best head shape produced during the entire steel shaft era. • Irons also gained new refinements during this period. Clubmakers began to give shape and form to the back of the iron head. The smooth backs found on most irons manufactured prior to 1930 were abandoned in favor of sculpted designs. The shapes were intended to weight the irons in such a way that they would be more playable, and the irons met expectations. • During the 1930s,

great improvements were made in the production of steel shafts. Better materials became available, and shaftmakers found better methods of heat treating along with other improvements in production. Steel shafts became the accepted standard. Most were made with step-downs (downward graduations in shaft diameter) but there was also a large demand for shafts with special designs such as spirals, ridges, bulges, and a variety of taper patterns. In most cases quality had to be sacrificed to produce the creative design. By 1942, however, True Temper had developed a shaft that was anything but a gimmick. Their Dynamic shaft, the most popular steel shaft in the history of the game, remains on the market today. • In 1931, the USGA broke from the R&A and established the size of golf balls at no less than 1.68 inches in diameter and no more than 1.55 ounces in weight. This lightweight "balloon" ball met with such protest that in 1932 the USGA kept the size but changed the weight to a maximum of 1.62 ounces. This standard was adopted by the R&A in 1952 and remains in effect today. • With improvements in the process of vulcanizing rubber covers and winding rubber around the core, balls were now going farther and lasting longer. Other changes were also taking place. In 1930, the square dimple, which resulted in a lattice or mesh pattern, was a popular cover design. In 1940 the round dimple began to displace the square dimple and soon became the best selling golf ball cover pattern.

PEAKHI PUTTER

Covered under a British design registration granted to Sidney Green in July 1933, the Peakhi putter is not only oversized, it has a one-inch gap between the vertical portion of the hosel and the blade.

JONES 7 IRON

In 1929, Bobby Jones ordered a "back-up" set of irons from Tom Stewart. Stewart made the clubs for Jones, but then produced a few unauthorized copies marked with Jones' initials "RTJ." This 7 iron, however, bears Jones's full name and Stewart's personal inspection dot.

BRACE DRIVER

This broad head driver was produced by Tom Brace and bears a UK design registration number that dates to 1933. The face is made from a thick piece of ivory inlaid with 9 wood dowels. The top of the head has a stylish concave shape.

MASTER 30 3 WOOD

Offered in 1931 and 1932 at $22.50 per club, MacGregor's Master 30 Model woods were once MacGregor's premier woods. The shaft is a Bristol Gold Label steel shaft with a black "Mac-Oid" finish. Mac-Oid was a variation of pyroxylin applied by a patented process. The head is persimmon but it, too, is covered with black Mac-Oid. The white face, the red Scruloc inserts in the face, and the white centerwedge backweight are all made from Mac-Oid. The crown, however, is inlaid with mother-of-pearl.

WILSON PUTTER

This circa 1930 rectangular mallet putter, attributed to the Wilson-Western Sporting Goods company, employs a flat shaft best described as a wooden slat. The shaft measures 3/4 of an inch wide and only 1/4 of an inch thick. As installed in this putter, the shaft is exceptionally flexible. The full brass faceplate and three lengths of brass inlaid along the top of the wood head serve as alignment aids and add to the beauty of this club.

JONES JANE PUTTER

After completing the Grand Slam in 1930, Bobby Jones relinquished his amateur status when he signed a promotional arrangement with A.G. Spalding & Bros. In 1932, Spalding offered the first Kro-Flite Calamity Jane putters modeled after the one Jones used. The example shown is an early prototype that never went into production. Unlike Spalding's production model Calamity Jane putters, this putter is not marked Spalding, it lacks "Jr." after Jones's name, and the flying crow logo is unlike any that appear on production clubs.

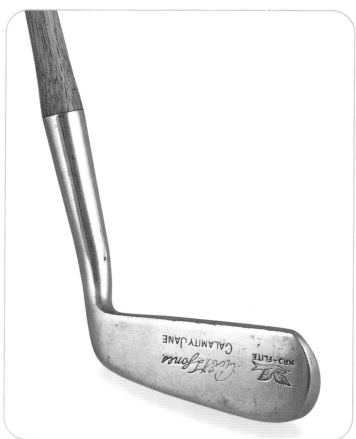

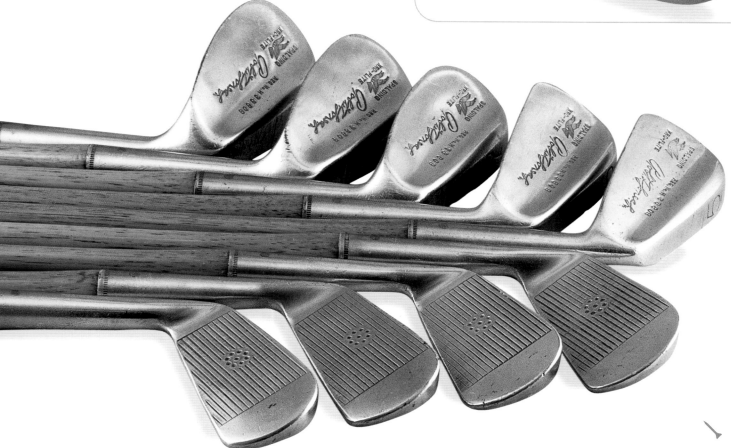

JONES IRON SET

Spalding's 1932 Spring and Summer catalog, the first to list "Robert T. Jones Jr." signature clubs, offered two different Jones model iron sets, but both came stock with steel shafts. The 1932 custom order set shown has original wood shafts and bears a matching custom number on each head.

RENWICK & JOHNSTON IRON

On May 5, 1932, William Renwick and Robert Johnston received a British patent that covered this club. Theirs was the first true cavity-back iron patented and produced. The patent also covered the short hosel that spirals around the steel shaft.

STREAM-LINE DRIVER

Produced by the Stream-line Golf Company of St. Louis, Missouri, this steel shaft circa 1930 metalwood has a triangular shape and a large, black, circular insert that was cast into the head. In the mid 1920s, Stream-line produced a hollow metalwood with a removable soleplate.

ADJUSTABLE CLUB

This unmarked wood shaft adjustable putter/chipper is usable either left- or right-handed. The loft adjusts by turning a screw in the back of the hosel. William Spiker's 1931 US patent covers an "adjustable short approach shot club or chipper" similar to this club.

CASH-IN PUTTER

From the 1930s to the 1980s, the Cash-In putter was one of the most popular putters on the market. Produced by A.G. Spalding and favored by many PGA Tour pros, the Cash-In was the creation of Robert Cash. The putter shown is one of Cash's original models, covered under his US design patent issued June 10, 1930. On October 29, 1940, Martin Flynn, assignor to A.G. Spalding & Co., received a design patent that replaced the Cash-in's original square edges with rounded edges.

GLOVER'S CLUB

Loosening the threaded nut atop the "toothed extension" raises the nut, allowing the blade to be repositioned. Turning the nut in the opposite direction lowers the nut, locking the blade into position. Edmond Glover, of Tenafly, New Jersey, received a US patent dated March 12, 1935, that covered this steel shaft mechanical iron.

PUTTER

Dating to the 1930s, this unmarked brass putter places the bulk of its weight directly behind the ball. The pyratone-coated steel shaft has a long black ferrule directly atop the hosel.

OGG-MENTED IRONS

By weighting the toe, Willie Ogg believed the entire blade became an effective hitting surface, not just one spot near the hosel. Both the Ogg-Mented 3 iron above left, first offered by Wilson Sporting Goods in 1933, and the Sarazen Hy Power 6 iron above right, made shortly thereafter, were produced under Ogg's patent.

PRO-SWING

Endorsed by Ernest Jones, the famous teaching professional, the Pro Swing practice club was produced in the early 1930s by the Pro Swing Golf Company of New York City. It consists of either a lead or brass ball on the end of a nine-inch spring attached to a hickory shaft. According to ads, swinging the Pro Swing would teach the golfer to drag the club back, shift his or her weight correctly, and put wrist snap into the shot.

DETROIT ADJUSTABLE

Produced by the Detroit Adjustable Golf Club Company, this circa 1930 steel shaft metalwood has an adjustable face. Turning the dial atop the head changes the angle of the face, so this club can function as a driver, brassey, spoon, or hyflight spoon.

STREAMLINER DRIVER

Aerodynamically designed to concentrate all the weight directly behind the ball, Streamliner woods were made in 1937 by MacGregor craftsmen and sold by Streamliner Golf Clubs, Sylvan Crooker, president. Streamliners were great in theory, but they did not work in reality (nor were they legal). Crooker received a 1937 US patent for this bullet-shaped club.

WHITE 8 IRON

This Jack White Gruvset iron was produced in the UK during the 1940s. The sole is both beveled and grooved, so the back of the blade simply rounds down to the leading edge. This sole design was first described in Walter Smith's 1924 US patent.

TOM BOY DRIVER

Walter Hagen International Tom Boy woods, which came in both men's and women's lengths, have three reinforcing metal inserts in both the top and bottom of the head. According to the 1935 Hagen catalog, these "laminating inserts" add considerably to the strength of the club. This head has the Hagen one-piece brass face insert and soleplate. The metal shaft is Hagen's Bi-Taper with "red oak tan Permo finish."

NELSON 8 IRON

MacGregor used this split back design in most of its Tommy Armour irons made between 1935 and 1967. This 1940s Byron Nelson iron has a steel shaft covered with green "Armour silver sheathing."

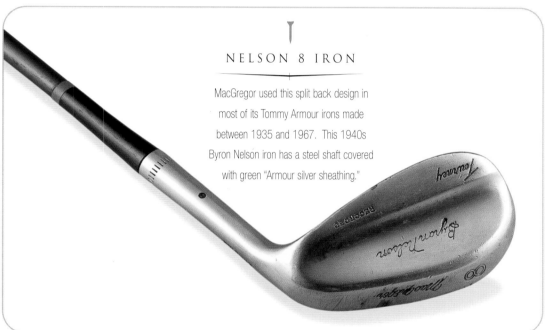

JONES 7 IRON

In 1939 Gerald Geerlings, assignor to A.G. Spalding & Bros., applied for a design patent to cover the fish scale face pattern found on this Spalding Registered Robert T. Jones Jr. 7 iron. A patent was issued on October 1, 1940. Such designs were used to make clubs more interesting and attractive, not necessarily better.

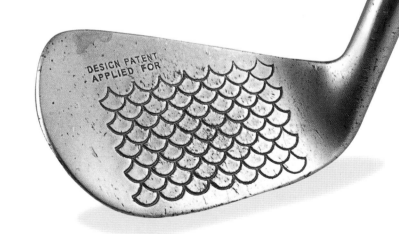

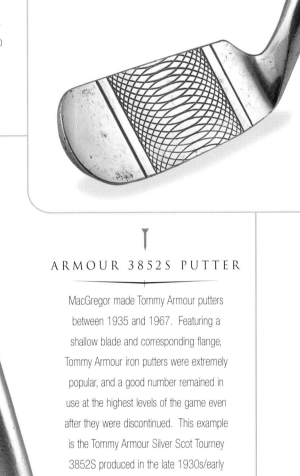

PAR-A-LEL 6 IRON

In 1933 Henry Davis, assignor to Mavis Machine Corp. of New York received a US patent for this club. Billings & Spencer Co. of Hartford, Connecticut, produced this club under license from Mavis Machine. The "6 spade mashie" shown is marked "Pat. Applied For."

ARMOUR 3852S PUTTER

MacGregor made Tommy Armour putters between 1935 and 1967. Featuring a shallow blade and corresponding flange, Tommy Armour iron putters were extremely popular, and a good number remained in use at the highest levels of the game even after they were discontinued. This example is the Tommy Armour Silver Scot Tourney 3852S produced in the late 1930s/early 1940s. It is modeled after the Spalding HB putter first offered in 1919.

LEVEL SHOT BRASSEY

Produced by the Level Shot Golf Club Company of Chicago, this circa 1930 brassie has a level inlaid into the top of the head. Installed at an angle to the top of the head, the level is placed so that the bubble will move between the two center marks only when the club is soled squarely on the ground.

STROKUM ADJUSTABLE

Marketed by the Strokum Manufacturing Company, the Strokum adjustable club was covered under 1941 and 1944 US patents issued to John Nilson. Simply push the spring-loaded head towards the hosel to rotate the head to a new loft. Each of the three sides of the head can function as a striking face.

BLOMFIELD ADJUSTABLE

This clubhead pivots on a spindle-like extension that projects from the shaft. Loosening the screw in the slot on the top of the head loosens the head so the golfer can change the loft. After the head has been repositioned, tightening the screw holds the head in place. The grip on this club can also move up and down to adjust the length. John W. Blomfield received a British patent on May 21, 1931, for this mechanical club.

DIRECT LINE PUTTER

This Crosby Direct Line putter features a
fixed alignment rod reminiscent of that on
both the Rudder putter (p. 121) and
Hardingham's putter (p. 85) produced
years earlier. The blade, however, is of
the traditional end-shafted style.

ALL AMERICAN METALLIC

This All American Metallic driver does not
have a crown. The side walls, however,
remain. Any golfer unable to use this club
with success had only to cut the shaft
down and move it to the kitchen—why
throw away a good soup ladle!

FAITH SPOON

Clubmakers have long recognized that the
cosmetics of a golf club can influence
sales. To this end, this Faith Super Flight
spoon has an aluminum face insert inlaid
with a copper winged golf ball.

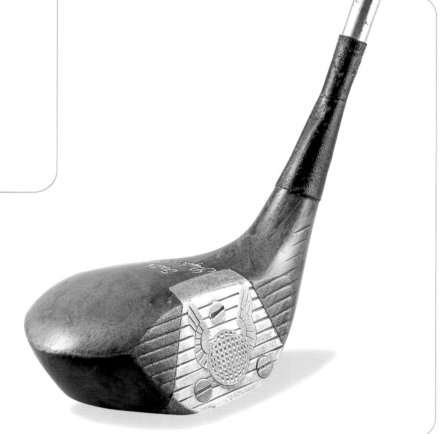

BULLS EYE PUTTER

The Bulls Eye putter was first produced by John Reuter Jr., while living in Sioux Ste. Marie, Michigan. In the early 1940s, Reuter moved to Phoenix and opened his Bulls Eye Putter factory. In 1968 Acushnet purchased the rights to the Bulls Eye for $250,000 plus a monthly/yearly retainer until Reuter's death in 1984. This Bulls Eye is a pre-Acushnet "Pat. Pending" model.

ARMOUR JUMBO

In 1939, MacGregor offered their first extremely deep-faced driver—the Tommy Armour Jumbo. It measured a full 2 inches in face depth. In 1941 they offered two jumbos: the Armour BJD (stiff shaft) and BJM (medium stiff).

WILSON R-90

Gene Sarazen, sometimes credited with inventing the sand iron, was but one of many who sought to improve upon Edwin MacClain's Sand Wedge (p.117). Sarazen, however, did design what is arguably the single most *popular* sand iron ever made —the Wilson R-90, first sold by the Wilson Sporting Goods Company in 1933. Before square or U grooves and lob wedges, early R-90s often sold for $300 to *players*.

PAR METL CLUBS

Par Metl woods and irons are made from brass with red fiber inserts riveted into place. The back of the head is hollowed out on both the brassey and the spoon. The 9 iron in the center has a regular smooth back.

NIAGRA CLUBS

William Wettlaufer's 1937 US patent covered the Niagara 7 iron and 3 metalwood shown. The iron back is filled with mercury (one Allen-screw has been removed to show the fluid), and the removable shaft is purposely bent near the hosel. According to Wettlaufer's patent, the mercury was used to "adjust...and effect a predetermined distribution of the weight." The removable shaft, held in place by a screw in the sole, was bent so the golfer could rotate the head relative to the center axis of the shaft in order to counter hooking, slicing, or hitting the ball on the toe or heel. The metalwood has a removable black plate that forms the crown. The plate is off, revealing two chambers and two sets of weights bolted in place. Removing two nuts allowed access to the weights, which could be increased, decreased, or shifted.

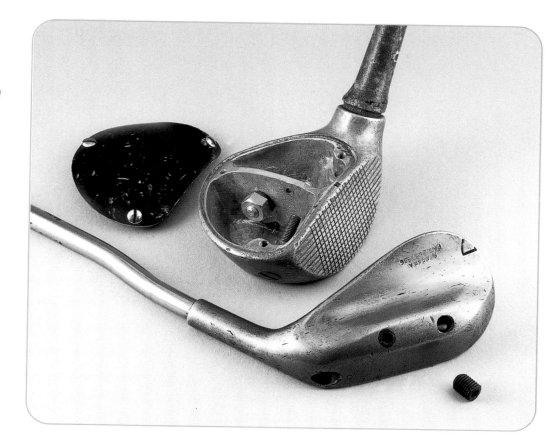

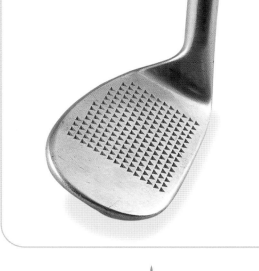

ARMOUR HOGAN 2 WOOD

MacGregor's 1941 catalog was the first to offer Tommy Armour Ben Hogan Model woods. The design was a good one. Armour Hogan model woods remained playable and sought-after until metalwoods overtook the market in the mid 1980s.

HOGAN 1 IRON

This is the very club Ben Hogan used on his approach shot to the 72nd hole at Medina during the 1950 US Open, which he won. The finish of Hogan's swing was captured in what has become the most famous photo ever taken of Hogan. Lost for several years, this iron was rediscovered and then authenticated by Hogan himself. MacGregor first produced this blade in 1949 as the Hogan Parmaker in their general line, not their pro line. This iron, however, was custom made for Hogan and marked "Personal Model," not Parmaker. It is now on display at the USGA.

KENNETH SMITH 99 IRON

In 1927 Kenneth Smith opened a full-service golf shop in Kansas City, Missouri. Since then, the Kenneth Smith name has become synonymous with custom-made clubs. Every club is assembled by hand to customer specifications. Every club is also marked with a unique production number. A call to the company revealed that this 99 iron (functions as a sand iron) was made in 1945 for Joe Novak, a Los Angeles pro.

SCHAVOLITE SPOON

Introduced in 1931, this Schavolite brassey has a head of Textolite—a type of rubber impregnated fabric devised and molded to shape by General Electric for Schavolite. The shaft was also molded in place.

SMILER PUTTER

Manufactured in Scotland, this Smiler putter gives the golfer a clear view of the blade by placing it well ahead of the shaft. Obviously this putter was not designed for those golfers who believe that keeping the hands slightly ahead of the ball is an important fundamental of good putting.

TRIJA CLUB

Made under a 1944 and 1945 US patent, Trija clubs often use one shaft and two iron heads to provide six clubs (accomplished by having two separate sockets on one head and rotating the shaft attachment 180 degrees), but additional heads were made. Shown are three irons, a metalwood and a putter, designed to fit a 2-piece shaft.

KLEERSITE 2 IRON

Kleersite irons were made by Wilson in 1938 and 1939. This Kleersite iron was made for US Open and US Amateur champion Francis Ouimet and bears his name.

ARMOUR 693 4 WOOD

Of all the wood shapes designed in the 20th century, MacGregor's Tommy Armour 693 model, first produced in 1949, may be the best. From driver to 4 wood, 693's were eminently playable at the highest levels and had classic lines. Their head shape was used by MacGregor in their 945, M43, and M85 Eye-O-Matic models (p. 156). Many other clubmakers found inspiration in the form of the 693 when designing their own clubs.

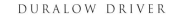

DURALOW DRIVER

Produced in the UK in 1931 by the Donaldson Manufacturing Company and covered under a 1933 US patent issued to William Hadden, Duralow metalwoods were designed to concentrate the weight behind the ball, provide greater top spin, and to lift a ball out of a "cupped" lie. Therefore, it has a brace extending straight back from the face, a high center of gravity, and nothing at all below the crown, except for the face and the brace.

Persimmon wood had been favored for clubheads since the turn of the century, so persimmon heads were nothing new. But, many of the persimmon clubheads made between 1950 and 1970 were something special. Years after they were produced, they were still considered to have just the right shape, look, and feel. During the 1970s and 1980s, anyone who looked into the bag of a PGA Tour pro often found one or more persimmon head woods made 20 or 30 years earlier. MacGregor produced the most popular models, but Wilson, Golfcraft, Hillerich and Bradsby, and others made a few models that remained in use at the highest levels of the game long after newer models were available. • Persimmon could chip, crack, or break during play. Clubmakers, therefore, also produced woods made from laminated wood, usually maple. These clubs were far more durable than persimmon but, over the years, were not as popular. They lacked the beauty, feel, and mystique attributed to a solid persimmon wood with its unique grain pattern and rich color. • The irons made during this era, like the woods, were classic in style. Most had a thin top line, a medium sole width, and a compact head. Some of the blade designs were popular not only in their day, they also remained popular for years in updated versions made by various clubmakers. • In 1966, Bob Mader introduced the first irons produced by the investment cast process. This construction method came to dominate a huge portion of the iron market beginning in 1968, when Ping began selling the Karsten I iron. The Karsten I, however, ushered in more than a new way to make irons. • Designed by Karsten Solheim, the Ping Karsten I iron was the first cavity back iron of the modern era. It quickly gained widespread acceptance when it was found that these irons were easy to hit, and they were forgiving. The investment cast process was adopted by many other clubmakers, and the Karsten I iron directly influenced the design of most heel and toe/perimeter weighted irons made for years thereafter. Karsten Solheim was also responsible for an entirely new style of putter. His multi-level back designs, heel and toe weighting, neck shapes, beveled edges, and radiused slopes, became the models which many other clubmakers followed to create their own lines of putters. Solheim's Anser putter continues as one of the most popular, if not the most popular, putter ever made. ✏ Croquet style putting, in which the golfer faces the hole and positions the ball between his or her feet, enjoyed a resurgence during this time. Hence, a number of small companies began to produce croquet style putters. In 1968, however, the USGA banned this method. **"Sidewinder"** putting, in which the golfer faces the hole but positions the ball outside his or her feet, was then tried as a substitute but with little success. • During this period, the dimple pattern on golf balls varied little among brands, and most balls were still made with elastic wound around a core. But, change was coming. In the early 1960s, both James Bartsch and Spalding marketed the first one-piece balls made from synthetic material. Bartsch's ball did not survive in the market for long, nor did the one-piece balls Faultless made under license from Bartsch. Spalding's ball was not any better, but Spalding persisted to create a solid core ball enclosed in a cover of polyurethane plastic. This two-piece ball, the Executive, was far superior and set the direction for future development.

BEE LINE PUTTER

The Bee Line putter, covered under Samuel Lombardo's 1969 US patent, concentrates all its weight directly behind the ball to help the golfer achieve a pendulum stroke.

RAY COOK M1-S

First produced in 1963 in San Antonio, Texas, Ray Cook putters quickly became popular at the highest levels of the game. By 1975 pros using Ray Cook putters had won the US Open, British Open, Canadian Open, PGA, Masters, and 140 other pro tournaments. These mallet putters, the first to feature narrow slots cut down into the head and through the head behind the face, aided alignment and improved response.

PUNCHIRON 9 IRON

Burke produced various Punchirons during the 1950s and 1960s. Shown is the model produced between 1953 and 1956. Burke first made clubs in 1910. In 1963 Victor Golf, who controlled the PGA Golf Company, purchased Burke. Thereafter, Burke was relegated to making general line clubs. Burke closed in 1977.

PRO ZONE 3 WOOD

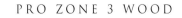

Dating to the early 1950s, this Golfcraft Pro Zone 3 wood has a persimmon head with an attractive laminated insert of thin strips of alternating red and white fiber. Acushnet/Titleist purchased Golfcraft's manufacturing facilities in 1968.

GARY PLAYER 8 IRON

Produced by Shakespeare during the mid
1960s, Gary Player Black Knight golf clubs
featured the black fiberglass WonderShaft.
Shakespeare promoted the WonderShaft
as an improvement over steel shafts just
as steel had been an improvement over
hickory. Dressed in black, Gary Player was
the perfect match for his clubs. Player,
however, found the fiberglass shafts
frustrating to use, so he had steel shafts
painted black installed in his irons.

CHICO'S TOMAHAWK

Chico Miartuz produced and sold his
Tomahawk putter independent of the main
golf companies. He did achieve some
success as his putter was used, however
briefly, by a few top professionals such as
Roberto De Vicenzo.

RINGER PUTTER

Looking like a perfect match for a 1957
Ford Thunderbird, this Ringer putter has a
vibrant turquoise head made from a molded
non-metallic substance. It has small lead
buttons in the heel, toe, and
center of the back.

CONFIDENCE 7 IRON

During the mid 1960s, Bob Mader pioneered the use of the investment cast process to make iron clubs. This was a huge innovation. Prior to Mader's work, all iron heads were drop-forged. After 1980 most irons were cast. In 1966 the first sets of Mader's Confidence irons, produced by his Mader Products, Inc., were available for sale at $300 a set - a *very* high price at the time. By 1973 his clubs enjoyed the highest of reputations. In the 1973 Los Angeles Open, 55 pros used Confidence irons.

MT M85 E-O-M DRIVER

MacGregor produced their winged MT M85 Eye-O-Matic woods between 1952 and 1955. The M85 Eye-O-Matic used the same driver head shape introduced in 1949 with the Tommy Armour 693 model, as did MacGregor's MT M43, Byron Nelson 259/663, and Armour 945 E-O-M—the driver Nicklaus used when winning most of his majors. During the 1980s, many top pros continued to use M85 drivers.

MIRROR PUTTER

The mirror atop this unmarked putter is positioned so the golfer can line up his or her putt by viewing the target in the mirror. In use during the 1950s-60s, the True Temper Meteor shaft in this club was advertised in 1959 as providing fine quality and step-down design at a medium price.

PENNA TP63 6 IRON

Toney Penna began working for MacGregor in 1934. In 1937 he signed Byron Nelson, Jimmy Demaret, and Ben Hogan as staff pros for MacGregor. Penna later became MacGregor's chief club designer and was responsible for much of what made the MacGregor clubs of the 1940s, '50s, and '60s the great clubs they proved to be. MacGregor's Penna TP63 irons were special order clubs produced in 1963. In 1967 Penna started his own golf company.

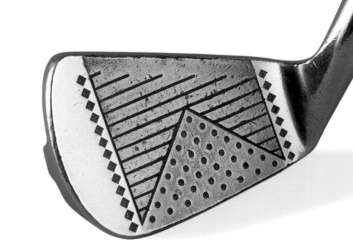

PALMER PUTTER

Wilson produced the Designed By Arnold Palmer putter (made both with and without the "Designed By") in 1962 and 1963. In 1963 and 1964 they made an identical putter, but without Palmer's name, marked "The Wilson 8802." The Designed By Palmer and 8802 putters quickly gained a devoted following and grew dramatically in price when it was noticed that such players as Lee Trevino and Ben Crenshaw were using these models during the height of their careers. Wilson then produced a number of 8802 remakes.

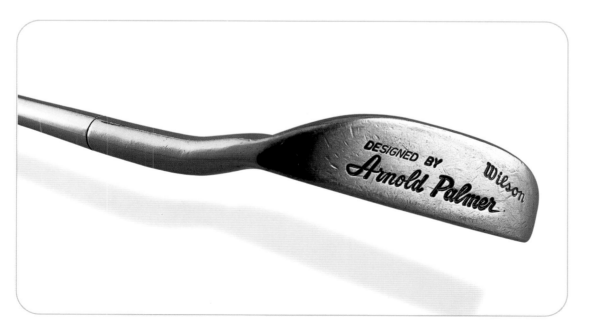

POWER BILT 5 WOOD

This Hillerich and Bradsby Power Bilt 5
wood, with two-tone fiber insert, matched
the 302 and 402 wood sets sold in 1956
and the 303 and 403 wood sets sold in
1957. It was offered as a single order
item as was a similar 6 wood.

BRANDING IRON

Produced during the mid-1960s by the
S&T Olympic Fields Putter Company, the
Branding Iron putter features a huge bend
halfway up the shaft. The head, however, is
set well forward, so the leading edge lines
up just behind the grip. In a 1966 ad, S&T
noted that the Branding Iron had just helped
win a tour championship and $20,000!

LINKSTER WONDER CLUB

Acccording to a 1961 ad, the Linkster
Wonder Club has 30 degrees of loft and
the length of a No. 1 iron. It was designed
to function as a 6 1/2 wood and lift the
ball out of the most difficult lies. Marketed
by the Frank Mitchell Co. of New Jersey, the
Linkster has bronze inlaid in an aluminum
alloy head and a hollow ground sole.

CONTINENTAL WOODS

For at least 4 years, from 1963 through 1966, Golfcraft offered their Continental woods in a natural finish, but only in limited numbers. These Continental fairway woods have the natural finish. A 1963 Continental advertisement states that only a few heads out of every thousand inspected had the grain, color, and quality to "show perfect" in a natural finish. Continental woods, with either steel or fiberglass shafts, were the most expensive woods offered by any major American golf club manufacturer. Orders took from 3 to 5 weeks to fill.

MANGRUM 8 IRON

In 1954 Golfcraft began using Glasshafts in their clubs. These shafts were actually fiberglass laminated to a thin steel core and were made in black, brown and silver gray. Golfcraft produced the Mangrum Glasshaft clubs from the mid-1950s into the 1960s. Lloyd Mangrum remains the most successful Canadian touring pro with 34 wins to his credit including the 1946 US Open. In 1968 Acushnet/Titleist purchased Golfcraft in order to make their own clubs.

CENTURION WOODS

Both of these distinctive drivers, produced by Steve Biltz, have circular toe and heel weights that were easily adjusted, allowing the golfer not only to change the swing weight but also the balance of the club. The driver above has a laminated maple head and was covered under a design patent issued to Biltz on February 7, 1967. The driver at left has a persimmon head and is the older of the two.

WILSON SAND WEDGE

When Tom Watson holed his chip from the high rough next to the 71st green at the 1982 US Open at Pebble Beach, defeating Jack Nicklaus in the process, he used a 1958 Wilson Staff Dyna-Powered sand wedge like the one shown. Watson's own club received a two-page spread in the Dec. 27, 1982, issue of *Sports Illustrated*.

NICKLAUS VIP 1 IRON

In 1967 MacGregor introduced the VIP line of clubs designed by Jack Nicklaus. The 1967-1968 model was solid and effective—Jack himself used the 1967 VIP irons for thirteen years during the prime of his career. Various models were made until 1980, the last year MacGregor produced the VIP by Nicklaus. Early VIP woods and irons used Tourney Taper Microstep shafts. These shafts appeared to lack step-downs but were advertised as having millions of "microsteps" invisible to the naked eye.

ZAHARIAS 7 IRON

Mildred "Babe" Zaharias was an All-American basketball player in 1930, '31, and '32. She won two gold medals in the 1932 Olympics in Los Angeles and set many track and field world records. In golf she won the 1946 US Women's Amateur, the 1947 British Ladies, and the 1948, '50 and '54 US Women's Open, the last championship coming after a cancer operation in 1953. Zaharias died from cancer in 1956 when she was only 42. The Associated Press named her Women Athlete of the Year six times and, in 1950, Woman Athlete of the Half Century. In 1947 Babe signed with Wilson. This Wilson Zaharias Dyna-Weight 7 iron is from 1954.

TOM BOY PUTTER

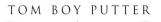

Joining the LPGA tour in 1959 at the age of 19, Kathy Whitworth did not cash a check in her first six months. In 1985, however, Whitworth won her 88th tour title, more than any other golfer in history, male or female, has ever won. In all of her 88 tour victories, Whitworth used a Walter Hagen Tom Boy putter like the one shown. Hagen also made a fiberglass shaft model.

TOP NOTCH 4 WOOD

Between 1950 and 1962, Wilson's Top Notch models were top-of-the-line, as expensive or even more so than the Staff models. This Top Notch 306 4 wood with persimmon head was made in 1958.

HAMMERHEAD PUTTER

The Hammerhead Putter was marketed by Sling-Master of East Orange, New Jersey. According to a 1957 advertisement, the Hammerhead putter cost $16.75 east of the Mississippi and $16.95 west of the Mississippi.

MT M75 11 IRON

MacGregor produced winged MT irons, designed by Toney Penna, throughout the 1950s. The plain face model shown was made from 1950 through 1954. The copper face "Colokrom" MT's were made from 1955 through 1957. The black face left hand "CF 4000" MT's were made in 1958-1959. The "75" in M75 identifies the shaft flex. M85 was firm (pro), M75 was medium firm (average), M65 was regular (senior), and M55 was flexible (ladies).

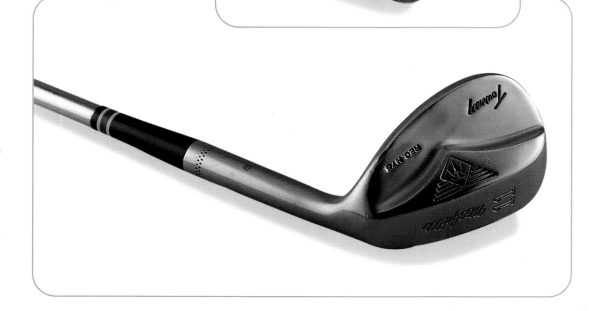

MOON CLUB

Alan Shepard was not only the first American to fly in space, he was the first human to play golf there! In 1971 Shepard stood on the moon with this most historic club, a 1962-63 Wilson Staff Dynapower 6 iron head altered to fit a collapsible shaft from a soil sampling tool, and hit two balls. He swung three times before he succeeded in sending his first ball a little ways off to the right. Shepard then dropped a second ball with which he connected. He initially estimated that the ball went "miles and miles," but he later revised his estimate to 200 to 400 yards. Even with the downward revision, Shepard's second shot remains a record for a 6 iron given a one-handed swing in a space suit. This club is on display at the USGA museum in Far Hills, New Jersey.

WIZARD 600 PUTTER

Designed by George Low and produced under both the Bristol and Sportsman brands, the George Low Wizard 600 was used by Jack Nicklaus to win 15 of his 20 major championships. The putter shown is Jack's own. The guide marks atop the blade were cut by Nicklaus soon after he started using this club. The first line was cut a little wide of the actual sweetspot, so he added the second line to frame the sweetspot. The Bristol/Sportsman George Low Wizard 600 putters were not popular when made in 1962, so few remain. Prior to the rise of Tiger Woods, the Sportsman model (which this club is) sold for $15,000 or more in Japan when flawless.

PING 69 7 IRON

In 1961 Karsten Solheim made the first Ping irons: the dual cavity back Ping 69 Ballnamic. He purchased the heads from Golfcraft and milled out the back in order to lighten the swingweight. Only 100 sets of the dual cavity back Ping 69 irons were made.

PROSONIC WEDGE

Pederson offered the brass head Prosonic irons, introduced in 1956, with either Rocket or Prosonic shafts. Pederson's Prosonic shafts have a reverse taper: the circumference is largest at the head and smallest under the grip. This brass Pedersen Prosonic pitching wedge has a Prosonic shaft.

WILSON STAFF 2 IRON

From 1956 to 1975, Wilson produced their Staff Model Dyna-power(ed) irons, complete with a drill through hosel filled with a rubber plug. The 2 iron below is the 1967-1968 model with an aluminum shaft Wilson offered between 1968 and 1971.

FIRST FLIGHT 7 IRON

The Professional Golf Company began producing First Flight clubs, via their First Flight Golf Co., in 1932. In 1974 Professional Golf became Pro Group. In 1983 Pro Group dropped the First Flight line. Shown is a 1965 First Flight Golden Eagle 7 iron.

PALMER 7 IRON

Arnold Palmer left Wilson in 1964 and started his own company. He contracted with Professional Golf to manufacture his clubs. In 1972 Professional Golf took over the Arnold Palmer Golf Company. Shown is a 1967 Palmer 5 iron.

KARSTEN I 7 IRON

Between 1968 and 1975, Karsten Solheim's Karsten Manufacturing Company produced Karsten I irons en masse. Viewed as a radical creation when introduced, the Karsten I's took the market by storm and, in tandem with Karsten putters, elevated Karsten Manufacturing into the top echelon of the clubmaking industry.

NICKLAUS 6 IRON

The first commercial sets of pro-line irons to bear the full "Jack Nicklaus" name were produced by MacGregor in 1980 (see p. 177). The iron shown, however, is from a custom set of pro-line Nicklaus irons MacGregor made in 1965-66 using Armour 985 blades. "Tourney" was a pro-line identifier.

TOP-FLITE 4 IRON

Spalding produced this Top-Flite iron in 1967 and 1968. It features a smooth back that quickly transitions to a thin topline. Thin toplines were a charactristic of many irons made in the 1960s.

SCOTCH BLADE 5 IRON

Hillerich and Bradsby produced several versions of their PowerBilt Scotch blade irons from 1966 to 1977 and again from 1983 to 1988. The example shown is a 1970-71 model.

HOGAN SABER 4 IRON

In mid 1954 a dissatisfied Ben Hogan destroyed the initial production run of his new golf club company—over $100,000 worth of equipment. He then designed the iron below, produced from 1955 to 1957.

LITTLE MAGICIAN

Measuring only 29 inches long, the Little Magician pendulum putter was made for croquet-style use. According to a 1962 ad, the Little Magician was sold by Home Industries of Jackson, Ohio. Both the head and shaft are made from aluminum.

KROLL PUTTER

The Kroll Putter was made for croquet-style use. The Kroll Putter Company was one of 30 to 40 small companies producing croquet-style putters that went out of business in 1968 when the USGA and R&A ruled that putting croquet style was illegal.

POWER PLUS 3 IRON

Power Plus irons, produced by Power Plus Products in Los Angeles, California, were designed to be shank proof. During the mid-1950s, when this 3 iron was made, Power Plus also made clubs for a game called "Plunkit," a game almost like golf except that a pitch into a canvas basket took the place of putting.

PING ANSER PUTTER

Created by Karsten Solheim in 1966, the Ping Anser Putter has proven to be one of the most popular putters of all time. It has not only been reproduced by Ping, the design has been widely copied (with only slight variations, if any) by many other clubmakers. Shown is the original model made from magnesium bronze and produced for 15 months in Scottsdale, Arizona. It now commands a price of $1500 or more.

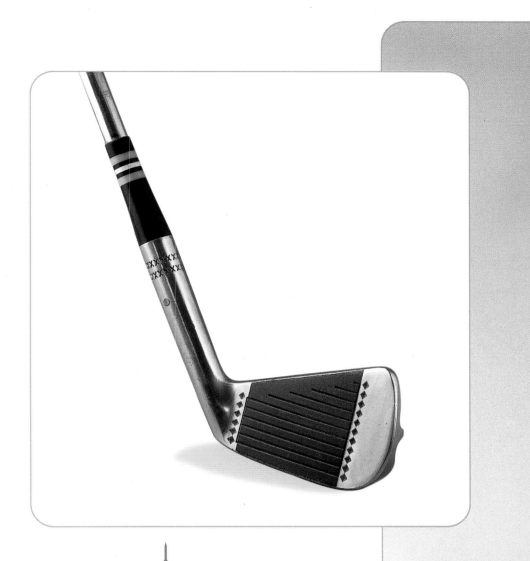

MACGREGOR FC4000 2 IRON

Between 1959 and 1965 MacGregor
offered a number of different iron models
with a black Flame Ceramic face, created
by spraying powdered ceramic material
onto metal at a high temperature. The
temperature was reportedly 4000 degrees,
hence the FC4000 designation.

MARBLE MAGICIAN

Sold in the mid-1960s by John Lambert's
Golf Enterprises based in Ohio, the Marble
Magician is a croquet-style putter. It has a
face inlaid with marble and a dramatic bend
located high on its aluminum shaft.

VELOCITIZED PT3W 4 WOOD

MacGregor made their Tourney Velocitized woods, with the half diamond top in 1958. PT3Ws came with Pro-Pel 3 shafts which, according to MacGregor, were "developed for the swinger or fine lady golfer." The heads were so desirable that, years later, better players often reshafted this model with a stiff shaft.

WOOD WAND PUTTER

Wood Wand putters were made in a few models, though all models had a wood and brass head, a wood shaft, and a solid wood grip formed to fit the hands. They were covered under two patents, issued to Howard Sasse in 1965 and 1966, and made by the Wood Wand Corp.

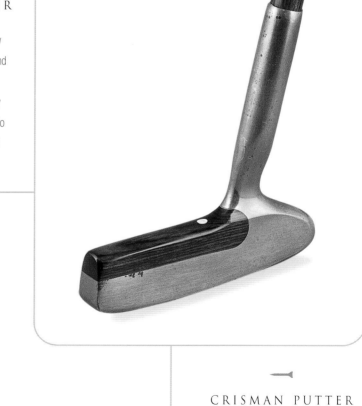

CRISMAN PUTTER

The Otey Crisman Golf Putter Company was founded in 1946 when Otey Crisman, trying to solve his putting woes, installed a hickory shaft in an aluminum mallet head of his own design. Crisman's hickory shaft putters quickly found a receptive audience and were used to win five Masters titles. As of 2002, hickory shaft Otey Crisman putters are still hand-crafted in Selma, Alabama, by Otey's son, Otey Crisman III.

CROOKSHANK 3 WOOD

J.H. Onion's Crookshank woods have a bend in the base of the shaft and corresponding neck in order to position the face on a direct horizontal line with the shaft. According to a 1965 advertisement, these British made clubs were available with prosimmonite, persimmon, or laminated heads. This 3 wood head is made from Prosimmonite, an injection molded plastic similar to that used in the MacGregor Constantwoods made in 1963-64.

RAKE PUTTER

According to a 1966 ad, the Rake putter would provide overspin by stroking the ball on the up-swing. Jones and Relfe, Ltd., of Montgomery, Alabama, produced the Rake.

PENNINGTON DUPLEX

This clubhead has two different faces, both for right-handed use. The faces are opposite each other but are on different axes, so each face has its own small sole. This club is marked "7" on one side and "8" on the other, along with "Penn-Smith, Patent Pend." etc. William Pennington of Salem, Indiana, received a US patent dated Dec. 17, 1968, for this club.

ONE-PUTT PUTTER

Designed for shuffleboard-style use, the One-Putt putter was covered under a US patent issued to Jerome McGranaghan of Virginia, on August 14, 1962. The roller in the sole enabled the club to glide smoothly across the ground.

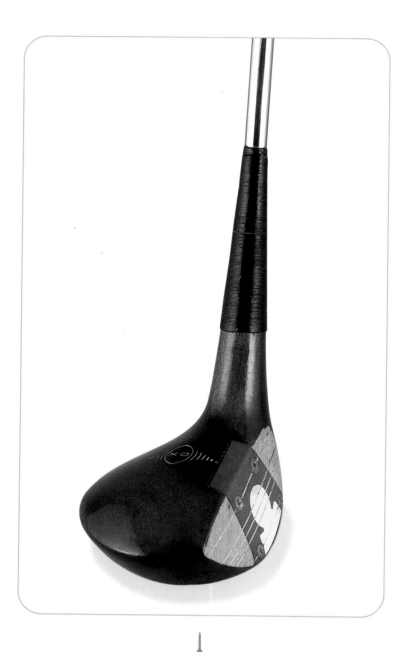

DX TOURNEY 5 WOOD

Between 1964 and 1966, MacGregor
made DX Tourney woods with "keysite"
inserts. The persimmon heads were
available in an antique burnished amber
or an antique rosewood finish (shown on
this 5 wood). Keysite inserts came in
different colors such as black with
yellow or black with red.

BAYMILLER PUTTER

John Baymiller of Lancaster, Pennsylvania,
received a 1970 US patent that covered
this flexible shaft putter. Because the
bottom third of the shaft has an extremely
small diameter, it is far more flexible that
the top two-thirds. Baymiller believed that
a shaft with a *uniformly* flexible portion near
the head would be more accurate for the
"delicate effort" required in putting.

SIDEWINDER PUTTER

When the USGA banned croquet-style putting, a number of golfers were left in the lurch. To compensate, a few golfers tried putting "sidewinder-style," in which the golfer still faced the hole but placed the ball outside of his or her feet. This method did not last, but the concept of lengthening the shaft and splitting the grip, shown on this circa 1970 Sidewinder 39-inch putter, gave rise to the long handle putters of the mid 1990s.

MICKEY WRIGHT DRIVER

Produced by Wilson in the mid 1960s, this Mickey Wright Champ laminated driver was a "general line" club. General line clubs cost less than pro line clubs. Mickey Wright, however, was anything but "general line." Born in 1935, Mickey Wright won both the US Women's Open and the US LPGA titles four times. Between 1956 and 1964, she won 63 titles, including 13 in 1963. Overall, she won 82 tournaments. Her swing was legendary.

PLUS 1 EQUALIZER

Founded in December of 1953, the Ben Hogan Company has enjoyed an enduring reputation for producing forged irons geared to the better player. The Hogan Plus 1 irons were offered in 1968, the Equalizer functioning as a pitching wedge.

1 9 7 0

GRAPHITE &

TODAY

TITANIUM

11

As golf entered the space age, clubmakers paid close attention to advances in physics, technology, and high-tech materials—especially graphite and titanium. • Graphite is made from extruded rayon fibers pyrolyzed at temperatures up to 5,000° F. until they become carbonaceous—hence the term "carbon-graphite." The first graphite golf shafts were created in 1970 by Frank Thomas while working for Shakespeare. In 1972, Tour pro Gay Brewer began using graphite shafts and claimed that this new lightweight black magic helped him drive straighter and fifteen or more yards farther. • Graphite shafts, however, had their weaknesses. It was the mid-1980s before graphite shafts achieved widespread use, and then primarily in drivers and fairway clubs. Steel-shafted irons are still the standard among PGA Tour pros because the bending profile (the way a shaft flexes) is not as consistent from one matching graphite shaft to the next as it is from one matching steel shaft to the next. Grahite-shafted irons, however, have achieved great popularity among amateur golfers (especially seniors and ladies) who desire lighter clubs which are a little easier to swing. • Metalwoods made from stainless steel took over the market in the 1980s. In 1995, influenced by advances in the aerospace industry, Callaway introduced the Great Big Bertha driver with an oversize head made from titanium. A new standard was born overnight. Titanium was so strong, durable, and lightweight that the head could be made nearly twice the size of a conventional wood, and the face was both strong and lively. Soon after the Great Big Bertha was born, it was surpassed in size. In 2001, with drivers of gigantic proportions looming on the horizon, the USGA proposed limiting clubhead size as well as the overall length of a club. • Traditional forged steel irons remained in production throughout this period, but cast heel- and toe-weighted irons won much of the market. A new method of clubmaking, however, was introduced in the late 1980s: the use of milling machines to make putters. • Originating from a rectangular block of metal, milled putters are either hand-milled or CNC milled. Either way, all milled heads are cut to shape by a machine. On a Computer Numeric Controlled milling machine, a computer controls each cut, and a clubhead can be produced, complete with all markings, in less than 25 minutes. On a manually controlled milling machine, a person operates the knobs that control each cut, and a single clubhead takes at least 4 to 5 hours to produce. If the head and hosel are milled as two separate pieces, as is normally done , they are fusion welded or wire welded together. • You can not tell a hand-milled clubhead from a CNC clubhead. Most hand-milled putters have hand-stamped scoring marks and identification letters, but so, too, do many CNC milled putters. They are often marked by hand in order to look hand-milled for marketing purposes. Compared to hand-milling, however, CNC milling is more accurate for reproduction. It can produce a single or an infinite number of identical copies. • During the 1970s, ball makers turned their attention to creating new patterns, sizes, and types of dimples. Balata rubber covers were being replaced with Surlyn, a thermoplastic resin devised in 1968. During the late 1970s and 1980s, balls were offered in a variety of colors such as optic orange and yellow, but color faded away. The biggest innovation was the move beyond the wound core to a molded solid core ball, be it made in one, two, or many layers. Today, the solid core ball dominates the market.

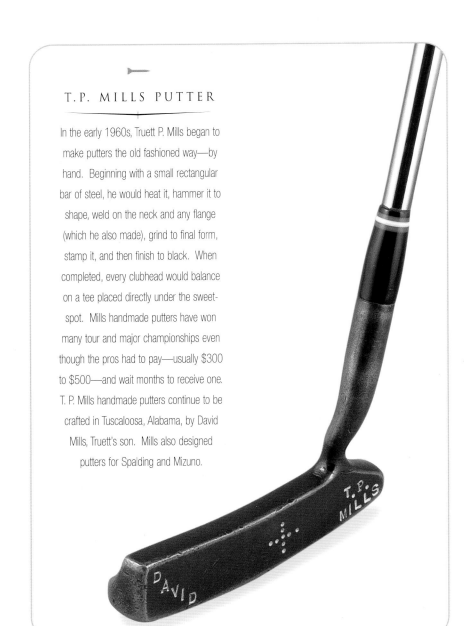

T.P. MILLS PUTTER

In the early 1960s, Truett P. Mills began to make putters the old fashioned way—by hand. Beginning with a small rectangular bar of steel, he would heat it, hammer it to shape, weld on the neck and any flange (which he also made), grind to final form, stamp it, and then finish to black. When completed, every clubhead would balance on a tee placed directly under the sweet-spot. Mills handmade putters have won many tour and major championships even though the pros had to pay—usually $300 to $500—and wait months to receive one. T. P. Mills handmade putters continue to be crafted in Tuscaloosa, Alabama, by David Mills, Truett's son. Mills also designed putters for Spalding and Mizuno.

BOMBSHELL DRIVER

Irons were first made from investment cast stainless steel in 1967, but it wasn't until Pinseeker introduced the Bombshell clubs in 1976 that metalwoods were made by the investment cast process. Pinseeker's initial stainless steel Bombshells, produced between 1976 and 1979, had alignment slots on the top of the head and a futuristic design patented by Edward Riley, one of Pinseeker's founders.

THE TEACH PUTTER

In 1988 the Teach putter was patented in the US by Joe Rango. The head is round, like a golf ball, except for a flat face and the sole, which is beveled for right and left hand use. The golfer would practice with the *round* side of the head, then switch to the flat face, shown, for regular play.

AIR-FLOW DRIVER

Made by Tru-Angle, the Air-Flow driver allows air to flow *through* its head. Behind the perforated face is a large, hollow cavity connected to an open channel that runs out the back of the molded head—all in the hope of increasing clubhead speed.

MACDOUGAL P-101 PUTTER

During the late 1970s, Stewart MacDougal designed a number of putters for the Ben Hogan, Arnold Palmer Golf, and Hillerich and Bradsby companies. The Ben Hogan Company, for whom MacDougal designed six wood shaft and six steel shaft putters, offered the P-101 putter.

TRU-BALL PUTTERS

Tru-Ball putters, complete with a weight port in the rear of the head, were patented by Anthony Carlino of New York. According to Carlino's January 25, 1972, US patent, the ball shape of the head would aid the golfer in visualizing his or her stroke, thereby increasing accuracy.

NEKLES DRIVER

In an effort to produce a persimmon head that would not crack in the neck, as sometimes happened during play, Kenneth Smith devised his Nekles wood. In 1976, Smith received a US patent for his club, but fewer than 250 were produced.

ONE-PUTT PUTTER

The One-Putt putter was covered under a US patent issued to Sonnie Perkins of Redmond, Washington, on January 4, 1977. According to his patent, Perkins designed this putter so a golfer could line it up from behind the ball and then maintain the established direction while moving into the normal putting position. The upper portion of the hosel is positioned at a right angle to the blade and has an alignment line that runs its length.

PREDATOR 3 WOOD

Made by Lynx between 1977 and 1982, Predator metalwoods feature a large walnut inlay in the back of an aluminum head. Predators were offered with either a straight or an offset hosel, as shown.

STRING FACE PUTTER

If you ever wondered what it would be like to putt with a tennis racket, this putter provides the answer! The face is tightly strung with the same kind of string used in tennis rackets. The head is unmarked, but it was made after 1973 when True Temper began printing their name below the last step-down on their shafts.

NICKLAUS LE 6 IRON

In 1981, MacGregor made 1,000 sets of irons—1 through SW—that were exact copies of the irons Jack Nicklaus used to win the 1980 PGA and US Open. These were the first commercially available pro-line iron sets to bear the full Jack Nicklaus name. MacGregor's suggested $1,000 retail price was quickly left behind as Nicklaus Limited iron sets were (for a time) resold for upwards of $10,000 in Japan. Witnessing MacGregor's initial success, many other club manufacturers jumped on the limited edition "collectible" bandwagon. This 6 iron is from set #467.

CENTERSHAFT 5 IRON

This 5 iron is part of a 3-5-7-9-putter set of clubs that, judging from a True-Temper mylar shaft band, appears to have been made in the early to mid 1980s. Lacking any identification beyond the number marked on each sole, these clubs represent an idea that was tried then quickly abandoned.

STABILIZER PUTTER

With a twin tube shaft that forks to enter the head at the toe and heel, this Bill Jed Stabilizer putter sought to provide a two-inch-wide sweetspot. Rawlings included this putter, with slight modification to the top line, as the "Stablizer I" in its 1984 product line.

CARBONEX 22 5 WOOD

In 1982 Yonex entered the golf market by introducing the black Carbonex II woods, the first woods made with all graphite heads. In 1984 Yonex produced their burgundy Carbonex 22 woods, made from over 30 layers of compression molded graphite around a urethane core. The graphite face was promoted as being five times harder than ordinary faces.

METALWOOD 1 DRIVER

Introduced in 1979, Taylor Made's Metalwood 1 exploded onto the golf world and led the entire market away from traditional woods. This was an incredible coup, as Taylor Made Golf was founded in 1979. Shown is an early model with the weight adjusting set-screw in the sole.

ACCU-FLO 4 IRON

Titleist produced cast stainless steel Accu-Flo irons from 1979 to 1982. With large sole and wide face, they were designed more for the needs of average golfers than for touring pros.

TAD MOORE PUTTER

Tad Moore began designing and creating clubs in 1963. This particular Tad Moore putter was hand milled by Tad in 1988 and submitted to Maxfli, which then hired Moore to design a complete product line. After forming his own company during the mid-1990s, Moore returned to doing design work for Maxfli as well as producing his own milled putters.

CARBONIRON 4 IRON

In 1984, Japan's Yonex introduced the first graphite head irons. When these irons, which have a metal sole, were constructed, each head was individually wrapped with more than 20 layers of carbon graphite and then molded under extreme pressure. This 4 iron has a Vortical steel graphite shaft.

TOP-FLITE MAGNA DRIVER

Spalding's Top-Flite Magna Oversize driver, produced in 1995-1996, complete with a graphite face and shaft, does not have a crown. It is very similar to the All-America metalwood shown on page 146, showing that old ideas often return in new products.

BETTINARDI PUTTER

Originally hired to mill putters for Ken Gianinni in the late 1980s, Bob Bettinardi went on to mill putters for Cameron, Titleist, Maxfli and others before producing his own line in 1998.

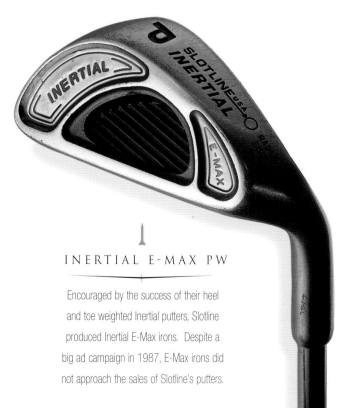

FEATHERLITE 5 IRON

In 1984, Dave Pelz Golf Research began offering Featherlite clubs. On average, these clubs were 1 1/2 ounces lighter than regular clubs and had an ultralight B-8 swingweight. Promising greater distance, accuracy, and ease of use, Featherlite clubs quickly grabbed market share, leaving many clubmakers rushing to produce their own models. By 1987, however, the Featherlite thrill was gone.

INERTIAL E-MAX PW

Encouraged by the success of their heel and toe weighted Inertial putters, Slotline produced Inertial E-Max irons. Despite a big ad campaign in 1987, E-Max irons did not approach the sales of Slotline's putters.

T-LINE DRIVER

PGA Golf/Tommy Armour Golf offered T-Line stainless steel metalwoods from 1983 to 1991. This example is marked "Tommy Armour Golf Company" on the sole and was made in 1985, when PGA Golf changed its name to Tommy Armour Golf Company, or shortly thereafter.

CAMERON PUTTER

So far in his young career, Tiger Woods has usually used Scotty Cameron milled putters. Both Cameron and Titleist (which has marketed most of Cameron's putters) have benefited greatly from the Woods connection. This putter sold for $750 in 1996 and is one of 960 copies of the putter Tiger used to win his third consecutive US Amateur. The Franklin Mint of clubmakers, Cameron has produced a number of limited run putters, most of which are based on Ping and T. P. Mills designs. Cameron also pioneered the $375 stainless steel divot tool. Experts agree, however, that the 25-cent aluminum divot tool should survive.

GREAT BIG BERTHA

Building on the popularity of their stainless steel Big Bertha driver designed by Richard Helmstetter and introduced in 1991, Callaway Golf introduced the Great Big Bertha in 1995. It had an even larger head and was made from titanium. It quickly became the most popular driver on the market and helped solidify Callaway as the largest golf company in the world.

FAT LADY SWINGS PUTTER

In 1994 Nick Price used one of these to win the PGA Championship. Almost overnight, Bobby Grace, the designer of The Fat Lady Swings, saw the production run of his putter jump from 12 to 250,000 pieces! When Price won the 1994 PGA, Grace did not have a single employee.

TITLEIST 975J DRIVER

The titanium Titleist 975D driver introduced in 1997 was well designed and well made. It proved to be an effective and popular club at the highest levels of the game. In late 2000, Titleist introduced the 975J. The most noticeable difference is that, at 312cc, the head on the J model is 52cc larger.

RADAR PUTTER

The Radar putter, a milled putter produced by the Ben Hogan Golf Company around 1990, has an open sole which provides the golfer with perimeter sole weighting.

SWILKEN Q2 8 IRON

Introduced in 1989 and offered in the US at $16,500 per set—woods, irons, putter, bag, shirt, shoes, etc.—Sandhill Swilken's Q2 limited edition set is the most expensive set of production clubs ever offered. The irons were made from the original propellers from the Queen Elizabeth 2 ocean liner. Production was limited to 7500 sets. Before long, full sets (sans shirt, bag, umbrella, etc.) were selling in the UK, home of Sandhill-Swilken, for only $2000—retail.

CLEVELAND 56° WEDGE

Cleveland Golf, formerly Roger Cleveland Golf Company, first produced the highly acclaimed Tour Action 588 irons and wedges in 1988. The black Melonite wedge shown was made from 1990 to 1992. (Melonite refers to a chemical treatment used to impregnate the metal.) During much of the 1990s, Cleveland wedges were the most used brand of wedge on the PGA tour.

HOLE-OUT PUTTER

This practice putter is designed *not* to hit the ball! Missing the ball with this club, however, is actually tough to do. The opening is just slightly larger than a ball, so only a perfect stroke will avoid contact. Robert Redkey, of Solvang, California, received a US patent dated March 29, 1990, for this club.

EXECUTIVE XE SET

Spalding's Executive XE clubs, produced between 1986 and 1988, were designed to provide the golfer with a totally integrated set of clubs, not a set of woods and a set of irons. One smooth, progressive clubhead shape extends from the driver straight through to the wedges. The driver, 3, 5, and 1 through SW are shown above.

EYE 2 L WEDGE

This is a beryllium copper Ping Eye 2 L wedge with box grooves. Introduced in 1985, Ping's L Wedge functioned as a third wedge, having more loft (61°) than a sand wedge. Ping's original box (square) grooves, also introduced in 1985, had rounded edges which met with opposition from the USGA and R&A, but not from golfers. Ping Eye 2 irons and wedges rank among the most popular clubs in the game.

ROLLMATIC STROKEMAKER

The Rollmatic Strokemaker was a practice putter intended never to leave the ground. The golfer was simply to roll the putter back and through, and the serrated roller would keep the club on line. The Strokemaker was patented in 1985 by Frederick Slagle and manufactured by Creative Sports Concepts of Madison, Ohio.

DOUBLEUP ZEBRA

Designed by Dave Taylor, Zebra putters
were first marketed by Ram in 1976 and
have enjoyed continued popularity. The fork
shafts in this DoubleUp Zebra, a teaching
aid putter, were patented in 1996 by
George Izett and Jay Ciccarone.

HOLLOW POINT DRIVER

Produced by the Bullet Golf Ball Company,
the Hollow Point driver was covered
under a 1994 US patent issued to Daniel
Sicaeros. After the USGA deemed the
Hollow Point to be non-conforming, Bullet
tried to make a conforming model by
installing a plate on the sole. The Bullet
HM-350 SL graphite shaft in this driver
was made by Aldila.

POWER CALIBRATOR

Covered under a 1989 US patent, Ram's
Power Calibrator iron is a "fitting club" used
to determine the desired shaft flex. The
golfer loosens the dial on the toe a little
more after each swing. When the lever on
the back moves to the "clear" position
during a swing, the number on the dial
indicated the flex was noted.

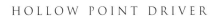

PELZ 3-BALL PUTTER

When Dave Pelz introduced this putter in the mid 1980s, the USGA declared it non-conforming because the head is longer than the face (which is nearest the shaft) is wide. Pelz then made a conforming model by switching the rear wing with the narrow face.

RESPONSE PUTTER

In 1986 Jack Nicklaus won his sixth Masters using MacGregor's new Response putter designed by Clay Long. Not only was this putter exceptionally large in size, so, too, was the public's response to Jack's victory—over 330,000 Response putters were sold within the next few years.

BIG BERTHA ERC II

The face of Callaway's titanium ERC II is thinner around the perimeter in order to increase the "trampoline" effect (coefficient of restitution) in the center where it contacts the ball. The increased trampoline effect the ERC II provided came under fire by the USGA, but was rule conforming by the R&A. New in 2000, the ERC II was named for Ely R. Callaway, Jr.

POWER POD DRIVER

In 1986, Jim Flood received a US patent for the Power Pod driver marketed by Orizaba Golf Products of San Diego. Like most clubs, the Power Pod, which also came in red, promised to hit the ball farther and straighter. Unlike most clubs, it was untraditional in almost every respect, including the ground glass mixed with epoxy resin that formed the head.

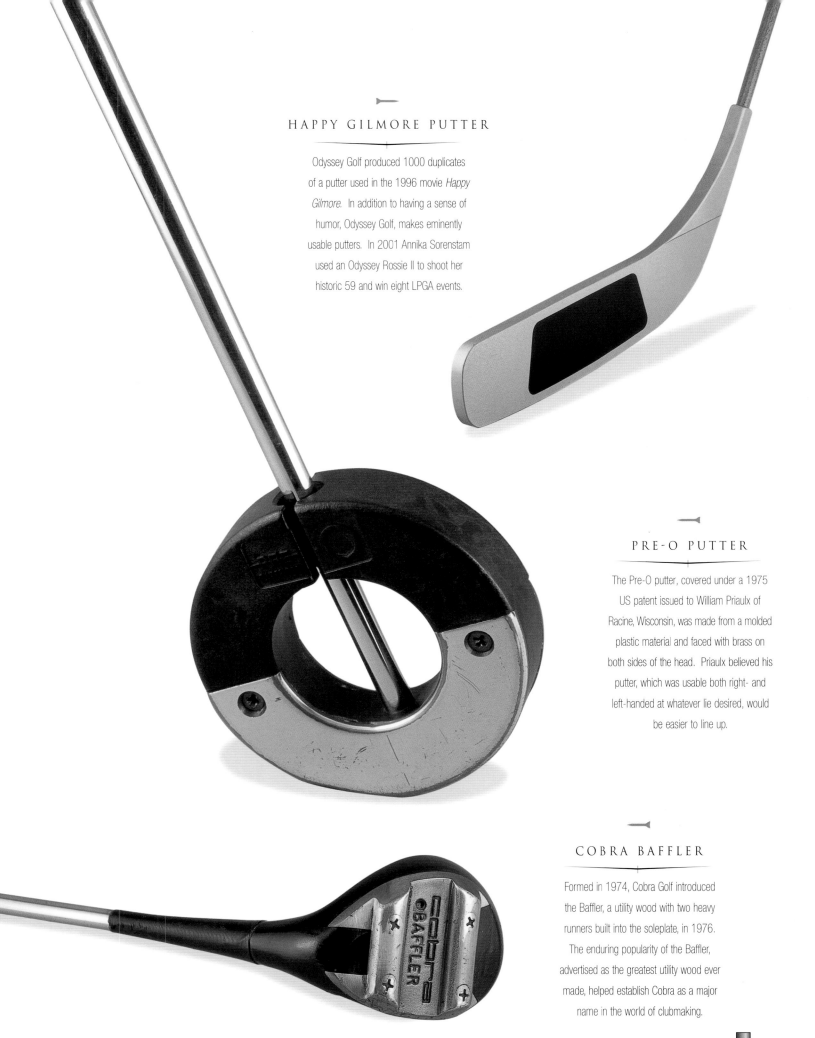

HAPPY GILMORE PUTTER

Odyssey Golf produced 1000 duplicates of a putter used in the 1996 movie *Happy Gilmore*. In addition to having a sense of humor, Odyssey Golf, makes eminently usable putters. In 2001 Annika Sorenstam used an Odyssey Rossie II to shoot her historic 59 and win eight LPGA events.

PRE-O PUTTER

The Pre-O putter, covered under a 1975 US patent issued to William Priaulx of Racine, Wisconsin, was made from a molded plastic material and faced with brass on both sides of the head. Priaulx believed his putter, which was usable both right- and left-handed at whatever lie desired, would be easier to line up.

COBRA BAFFLER

Formed in 1974, Cobra Golf introduced the Baffler, a utility wood with two heavy runners built into the soleplate, in 1976. The enduring popularity of the Baffler, advertised as the greatest utility wood ever made, helped establish Cobra as a major name in the world of clubmaking.

WILSON INVEX DRIVER

In 1996 and 1997 Wilson produced two versions of their Invex driver. The Bi Metal version had a stainless steel head and titanium hosel; the titanium version was all titanium. The Bi Metal example shown has a Wilson Firestick 2.8 graphite shaft.

LIL' DAVID SLINGER SW

Lil' David Slinger irons were made during the mid-1970s. According to a 1975 ad, the straight top of the blade produced automatic alignment, the curved sole offered less drag from divots, and the face provided a larger hitting area with a lower center of gravity.

HICKORY STICK WEDGE

Callaway Hickory Stick, USA was created in 1982 when Ely Callaway purchased the rights to the steel core "hickory stick" shaft and began selling putters and wedges. The company grew, producing irons then woods. The name was changed to Callaway Golf in 1988 when Callaway began using shafts other than steel core hickory.

MIZUNO MP-14 1 IRON

During the mid-1990s, Japan's Mizuno rose to prominence on the PGA Tour due largely to their forged MP-29 irons (introduced in 1993) and similar MP-14 irons (introduced in 1995) modeled after Hogan's mid-1950s Saber irons (see p. 165). Mizuno added the MP-33 model, a refinement of the MP-14, in 2000.

ADAMS TIGHT LIES

In 1995 Barney Adams introduced his Tight Lies fairway wood. Unlike other clubs, the sole is wider than the top of the head. Adams's club met with such success that within a few years he had turned his local clubfitting business into a major clubmaking company.

CLOSAR PUTTER

The Closar Putter, introduced at the 2002 PGA show in Florida, was created and patented by David Hoare of Las Vegas, Nevada. It is designed to produce a pendulum stroke and resist twisting on off-center hits. The head is made of milled aluminum with a copper face insert. (The back of the head is shown.) Closar Golf is located in Rancho Cucamonga, California.

PING TiSI TEC DRIVER

Made using Ping's Chemical Milling Technology and variable face thickness design, the 323cc titanium TiSI driver provides the maximum spring effect allowed by the USGA. Four out of the top five finishers at the 2001 World Long Drive Championship used a Ping TiSI Tec driver.

DOUGLASS PUTTER

Complete wiith a heel and toe weighted graphite composite head, a Surlyn face insert, and a painted metal shaft, the Douglass putter was covered under a January 1992 US patent issued to Michael Douglass of Wheatridge, Colorado. This modernistic putter did not receive much notice, its stealth-like looks apparently sneaking it in under the golfer's radar.

ULTRAMID DRIVER

According to Cobra ads, the head on Cobra's Ultramid driver was made from the same thermoplastic material developed by scientists for the bulletproof vest industry. Ultramid heads, however, were made from an injection molded polycarbonate and were prone to cracking, so Cobra made them for just one year—1990. John Daly used an Ultramid driver to win the 1991 PGA Championship.

ADVANCE PUTTER

In December of 1970, Vance Elkins of Freehold, New Jersey, began his search for the perfect putter. After much observation, he estimated that 70% of the golfers he tested aimed their putters about two degrees off-line to the right. So, he created his Advance Putter in an attempt to improve the golfer's alignment. Elkins would custom angle the lines across the top of the putter to correct for the individual player's particular deficiency. The Advance won such immediate acclaim from a number of touring pros that *Golf Illustrated* featured it on their August 1971 cover.

BROWNING 500 6 IRON

Originally founded in the late 1800s as a maker of firearms, Browning branched into the golf market in the mid 1970s. Many of their earlier irons have extremely low profile blades similar to that of the Browning 500, made between 1981 and 1984. In 1987 Browning sold its golf division to UT Golf, based in Salt Lake City, Utah.

NIKE 350cc DRIVER

In 2000, after Tiger Woods won four major championships in a row using a Nike golf ball, Nike decided to enter the golf club market. However, it wasn't until 2002 before Nike offered their forged irons and titanium metalwoods for sale to the general public. Rather than rush a product to market, Nike chose to make continuing improvements to their clubs prior to their introduction. It was a prudent policy: David Duvall won the 2001 British Open using Nike prototype irons, and early in 2002 Tiger Woods switched to a Nike driver.